Winning TOEFL

PAGODA LANGUAGE EDUCATION CENTER

Reading Step 1

Copyright © 2009 by **PAGODA Books**

All rights reserved. No part of this publication may be reproduced, stored in a retrieval system, or transmitted, in any form, or by any means, electronic, mechanical, photocopying, recording or otherwise, without the prior written permission of the copyright holder and the publisher.

Published by PAGODA Books
PAGODA Books is the professional language publishing company of the **PAGODA** Education Group.
19F, PAGODA Tower, 419, Gangnam-daero,
Seocho-gu, Seoul, 06614, Rep. of KOREA
www.pagodabook.com

First published 2009
Fourteenth impression 2024
Printed in the Republic of Korea

ISBN 978-89-6281-057-8 (13740)

Publisher | Kyung-Sil Park
Writer | PAGODA Language Education Center

A defective book may be exchanged at the store where you purchased it.

Winning TOEFL

Reading Step 1

Wit & Wisdom

WINNING TOEFL READING

Introduction to iBT TOEFL

iBT TOEFL (internet-based TOEFL) is designed to measure how well non-native speakers of English read, listen, speak and write in English. The test has four sections; reading, listening, speaking, and writing. Each section of the test is worth 30 points and the highest possible score on the iBT is 120 points (30 points x 4 sections). Most questions are worth 1 point each, but some of the questions in each section are worth more than 2 points.

 → For more information, visit the ETS Web site (www.ets.org).

Reading Section

(1) About the passages

In the reading section, test takers will be asked to read 3 or 5 passages. Each passage consists of 600~700 words. The test time differs according to the number of the passages given.

Number of Passages	Part & Passages			Test Time
3	Part I 1 Passage	Part II 2 Passages		60 min
5	Part I 1 Passage	Part II 2 Passages	Part III 2 Passages	100 min

The passage types are:

- Exposition: a type of writing that gives information about a topic
- Argumentation: a type of writing that develops a topic in a persuasive or logical way
- Narrative: a type of writing that describes a historical or biographical event

(2) About the questions

Each passage includes 12~14 questions. The questions test student's ability in the following areas:

- Basic comprehension: understanding vocabulary, pronoun usage, identifying true or false information
- Reading to Learn: recognizing sentence structure, summarizing
- Inferencing: implying, recognizing the writer's purpose

To test these areas, 10 question types are used in the iBT TOEFL reading section.

Question Type	Explanation	Number of Questions	Related Unit
Basic Comprehension			
Vocabulary	Choose the word that is closest in meaning to the word that appears in the passage.	4~5	Unit 1
Pronoun	Identify the word to which a pronoun is referring.	0~1	Unit 1
True Information	Choose a sentence that is true according to the passage.	2~4	Unit 2
False Information	Choose a sentence that is NOT provided or NOT true according to the passage.	1	Unit 2
Sentence Simplification	Choose a sentence which is closest in meaning to the sentence that appears in the context.	1	Unit 3
Inferencing			
Inference	Draw an inference from the passage by choosing an answer that is not actually stated in the passage but is implied or can be inferred.	0~1	Unit 4
Rhetorical Purpose	Identify why the author has mentioned something in a certain way.	2	Unit 5
Insert text	Insert a sentence into the most appropriate place in the passage.	1	Unit 6
Reading to Learn			
Categorization	Categorize related information from the passage.	0~1	Unit 7
Summary	Choose the sentences that best summarize the entire passage.	0~1	Unit 8
Total		12~14	Actual Test

Winning TOEFL Reading Series

This is the first reading book in the *Winning TOEFL* series. It has eight units and each unit includes four passages. This book is for the students who are at the beginner level, so the passages are shorter (200 words on average) and easier than the original passages seen on the actual TOEFL.

Each unit consists of:

Introduction ➔ Practice 1, 2 ➔ Test 1, 2

Each section has the following subsections.

Introduction

(1) Search! Search!

Students are encouraged to find some information about the topics on the cover page of each unit using the Internet. This part will give students the opportunity to become familiar with the topics before they actually read the passages in the Practice and Test sections of each unit.

(2) Target iBT TOEFL questions

This part introduces one or two of the iBT TOEFL question types. Each unit focuses on the following iBT TOEFL question types:

Unit	Question Types
Unit 1	Vocabulary Questions Pronoun Questions
Unit 2	Finding True Information Questions Finding False information Questions
Unit 3	Sentence Simplification Questions
Unit 4	Inference Questions
Unit 5	Rhetorical Purpose Questions
Unit 6	Insert Text Questions
Unit 7	Categorization Questions
Unit 8	Summary Questions

The question types introduced in this part will be practiced repetitively in the following subsections of each unit.

WINNING TOEFL READING

Practice 1, 2

(1) Warm Up
This part functions as a pre-reading activity. Students are required to reflect on their prior knowledge of the topic by answering the questions. They are also asked to guess what the passage is about using the words on the list. This section will help students practice essential pre-reading skills such as *skimming* and *scanning*.

(2) Read the passage
This section provides a passage (about 200 words) for reading. Students are encouraged to reduce their reading time by keeping track of it.

(3) Target iBT TOEFL Questions
In this part, students can practice the target question types that they were introduced to at the beginning of each unit.

(4) iBT TOEFL Vocabulary
This section lists essential expressions that appear in the reading passage. Students are asked to match the target words with their correct meanings.

(5) Wrap Up
In this section, students can review the expressions introduced in the iBT TOEFL Vocabulary section. This section also provides a summary (note) of the passage of each practice. Students can check their overall understanding of the passage by figuring out the main ideas and the organization of the passage.

Test 1, 2

This section introduces two passages that include various kinds of iBT TOEFL questions. Students can check their comprehension with these questions.

Following Unit 8, an actual test is provided.

Actual Test

Five passages are provided as an actual test. Students will be able to check their overall understanding of many iBT TOEFL questions that they were introduced to in the previous units. The test passages contain more expressions and are slightly more difficult than the passages in each unit.

WINNING TOEFL READING

Contents

- **Introduction to iBT TOEFL** — 4
- **Winning TOEFL Reading Series** — 6

Unit 1	Environment	10
Unit 2	History	24
Unit 3	Biology	38
Unit 4	Anthropology	52
Unit 5	Literature	66
Unit 6	Astronomy	80
Unit 7	Arts	94
Unit 8	Architecture	108

- **Actual Test** — 122

Passage 1	Caffeine	124
Passage 2	Mad Cow Disease	127
Passage 3	The Placebo Effect	130
Passage 4	Printing Systems	133
Passage 5	Musicals	136

- **Answer Keys**
- **MP3 files** ➪ www.pagodabook.com

UNIT 01 Environment

•• Search! Search!

Find out about the topics using the Internet.
Glaciers, Urban Heat Islands, Tornadoes, Tree Removal

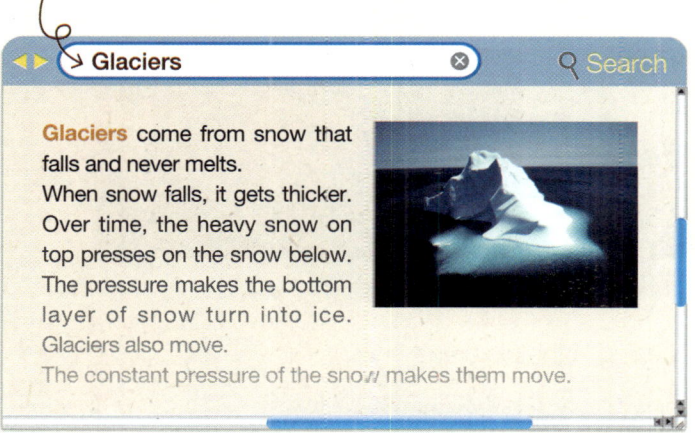

•• Target iBT TOEFL Questions

Vocabulary Questions

The word _____ in the passage is closest in meaning to…

Pronoun Questions

The word it / they / them / their in the passage refers to…

Practice 1

Warm Up

1 Can you guess what's happening in the pictures?

2 Think about life without trees. What would it be like?

Read the Passage

Tree Removal

Forests are removed so the land can be used for other purposes. One of the purposes is farming. Trees are also removed to make paper and building material. Tree removal causes many problems for the environment.

Many species of plants and animals live in forests. When forests are removed, these species lose their homes. Over time, plants and animals disappear. The trees in forests can also keep water in the ground. Without these trees, the land cannot hold water. This means it becomes drier than normal. When there is a lot of rain, the ground can't hold the extra water. This can cause a flood. A flood is an overflowing of water onto the ground.

Currently, the tropical rainforests are disappearing quickly. By the year 2030, eighty percent of the world's rainforests will disappear. To save the forests, we must stop removing trees.

* species: a group of plants or animals

Target iBT TOEFL Questions

1 The word their in the passage refers to
   Ⓐ animals   Ⓑ forests   Ⓒ species

2 The word disappear in the passage is closest in meaning to
   Ⓐ die   Ⓑ leave   Ⓒ change

3 The word hold in the passage is closest in meaning to
   Ⓐ have   Ⓑ own   Ⓒ store

4 The word it in the passage refers to
   Ⓐ land   Ⓑ water   Ⓒ rain

iBT TOEFL Vocabulary

Fill in the blanks with the appropriate words.

1	_____	**v** to take something away
2	_____	**n** the reason for doing something
3	_____	**adj** usual, typical
4	_____	**adv** now, at the present time
5	_____	**v** to make something happen
6	_____	**v** to stop existing

- purpose   • currently   • cause
- normal   • disappear   • remove

Environment •• 13

Wrap Up

A Complete the sentences with the appropriate words.

- removed
- currently
- purpose
- cause
- normal
- disappeared

1 Cars and factories _____ air pollution.

2 Nearly 500 houses were destroyed for the _____ of development.

3 Some countries _____ suffer from a lack of drinking water.

4 The unnecessary items were _____ from the list.

5 Tornado activity has been higher than _____ this year.

6 Dinosaurs _____ long ago.

B Complete the summary of the passage <Tree Removal>.

Forests are r_____ for farming, or for making paper and building materials. However, this causes many p_____ for the environment and can even cause a f_____. It also makes many plants and animals d_____ by destroying their homes. To avoid such negative effects, tree removal must be stopped.

Practice 2

Warm Up

1 Go through the passage quickly to find these words. Use what you know about these words to guess the topic.

- tornadoes
- destroy
- speeds
- damage

2 Identify the topic and read the passage quickly. What do you think the passage is about?

- An overview of tornadoes ○
- The speeds of tornadoes ○

Read the Passage

Your time (1st): ____ min, (2nd): ____ min

Tornadoes

Tornadoes are the most dangerous storms in the world. They begin with a thunderstorm. Tornadoes happen when two opposite types of air meet during a thunderstorm. If cool, dry air meets warm, humid air, the storm becomes unstable. Then, if the wind changes direction, the air starts to rotate.

The rotating air gets faster and stronger. It forms a column. The column stretches from the thunderstorm to the ground. Tornadoes look like long fingers reaching the ground from a storm. In seconds they can destroy houses, schools, farms and cars.

Tornadoes move at speeds between 100 and 500km per hour. Tornadoes are usually about 180 to 270 meters wide. They can last from a few seconds to several hours. Tornadoes are classified by the damage they cause. The lowest strength tornadoes are "F0". These cause only minor damage to the outside of trees and buildings. The strongest tornadoes are "F5". These completely destroy houses and throw large vehicles through the air.

Environment •• 15

Target iBT TOEFL Questions

1. The word opposite in the passage is closest in meaning to
   - Ⓐ unique
   - Ⓑ common
   - Ⓒ different

2. The word unstable in the passage is closest in meaning to
   - Ⓐ unsafe
   - Ⓑ changeable
   - Ⓒ huge

3. The word It in the passage refers to
   - Ⓐ thunderstorm
   - Ⓑ wind
   - Ⓒ rotating air

4. The word minor in the passage is closest in meaning to
   - Ⓐ little
   - Ⓑ unimportant
   - Ⓒ serious

5. The word completely in the passage is closest in meaning to
   - Ⓐ totally
   - Ⓑ usually
   - Ⓒ actually

iBT TOEFL Vocabulary

Fill in the blanks with the appropriate words.

#		
1	_____	**v** to lengthen or widen
2	_____	**v** to spin around a center
3	_____	**v** to damage something
4	_____	**adj** contrary, different
5	_____	**v** to organize by class
6	_____	**n** power, energy, force

- rotate
- opposite
- destroy
- classify
- strength
- stretch

Wrap Up

A Complete the sentences with the appropriate words.

- rotates
- opposite
- destroyed
- classified
- strength
- stretches

1 The hurricane _____ over 1400 houses.

2 The desert _____ from the Andes to the Pacific.

3 The Earth _____ every 24 hours.

4 The virus can be _____ into three groups.

5 The twins are completely _____ in behavior and attitude.

6 The _____ of bamboo increases with age.

B Complete the summary note of the passage <Tornadoes>.

Paragraph 1: How tornadoes are formed
- the most d_____ storms
- formation: a thunderstorm → two o_____ types of air meet
  → wind changes direction → the air starts to r_____
  → the rotating air gets faster and s_____

Paragraph 2: Characteristics of tornadoes
- Speed: ― km/h
- Width: ― meters
- Strength: F____ ~ F____

Test 1

Glaciers

Glaciers come from snow that falls and never melts. When snow falls, it gets thicker. [■A] Over time, the heavy snow on top presses on the snow below. [■B] The pressure makes the bottom layer of snow turn into ice. [■C] Glaciers also move. [■D] The constant pressure of the snow makes them move.

Glaciers move like slow rivers of ice. It can take thousands of years for a glacier to move a few meters. However, they make important changes to the land. As glaciers move, they push and cut the rock and dirt around them. Glaciers have made some of the world's most amazing valleys and rock formations.

Most glaciers are located near the North and South Poles of the Earth. Most continents have glaciers. Even Africa has glaciers! However, Australia does not have any glaciers. Glaciers cover ten percent of the Earth. Some are the size of a soccer field. Others are over one hundred kilometers long.

* **pressure:** force applied over a surface

| It snows. | The layers of snow turned into ice. | It starts over. |

<The formation of glaciers>

1 The word turn in the passage is closest in meaning to

Ⓐ change Ⓑ twist Ⓒ circle Ⓓ pour

2 The word constant in the passage is closest in meaning to

Ⓐ tough Ⓑ regular Ⓒ continuous Ⓓ big

3 Look at the four squares [■] that indicate where the following sentence could be added to the passage.

This process goes on for millions of years before ice forms.

Where would the sentence best fit?

4 The word them in the passage refers to

Ⓐ rivers   Ⓑ glaciers   Ⓒ mountains and valleys   Ⓓ rock and dirt

5 The author mentions that Even Africa has glaciers! in order to

Ⓐ emphasize that most continents have glaciers
Ⓑ show that Africa has glaciers
Ⓒ compare Australia and Africa
Ⓓ give an example of a continent that has glaciers

6 The word Others in the passage refers to

Ⓐ North and South Poles   Ⓑ continents   Ⓒ Earth   Ⓓ glaciers

7 According to the passage, which of the following is NOT true of glaciers?

Ⓐ They were originally snow.   Ⓑ They move slowly over time.
Ⓒ Not all the continents have them.   Ⓓ They form a river.

 **Glacier Facts**

- Presently, about 10% of the Earth's land area is covered with glaciers.
- During the last Ice Age, glaciers covered about 32% of the land.
- If all of the land ice melted, the sea level would rise more than 70 meters.
- Glaciers store about 75% of all the fresh water in the world.

source: www.noaa.gov

Test 2

Urban Heat Islands

Temperatures in cities are higher than temperatures in the countryside. Researchers call cities "urban heat islands." Human activity is the cause of this extra heat. Human activity includes driving cars and operating factories. Home heating and air conditioning also create heat in cities. In the summer, air conditioning systems actually make the outside air of cities hotter. The amount of heat made by people in cities is similar to the heat of the sun.

Another cause of high temperatures in cities is the material used for roads and buildings. Roads are made of asphalt. Sidewalks are made of concrete. [■A] Tall buildings are made of stone, steel, and glass. [■B] All of these materials hold heat longer than natural materials hold heat. [■C] Human-made materials also hold less water than trees and land hold. When water dries from heat it is called "evaporation". [■D] Evaporation cools the temperature of the air. In cities there is less water available to evaporate. This means less cooling of the air. Less evaporation and more heat held in urban materials means hotter cities.

* urban: related to a city

1 The word create in the passage is closest in meaning to

Ⓐ make　　　Ⓑ invent　　　Ⓒ miss　　　Ⓓ take

2 Why does the author mention the heat of the sun in paragraph 1?

Ⓐ To show how heat is made in cities
Ⓑ To compare the heat on the Earth with the heat of the sun
Ⓒ To give an example of other hot places
Ⓓ To emphasize the amount of heat made by people in cities

3 Which of the following is NOT mentioned as a cause of urban heat islands?

Ⓐ home heating   Ⓑ cars   Ⓒ body heat   Ⓓ asphalt

4 Look at the four squares [■] that indicate where the following sentence could be added to the passage.

Natural materials include trees, plants, and dirt.

Where would the sentence best fit?

5 According to the passage, which of the following is true of temperatures in cities?

Ⓐ Air conditioners keep city air cooler.
Ⓑ Buildings reflect heat.
Ⓒ Evaporation warms the air in cities.
Ⓓ Driving cars can raise the temperature of a city.

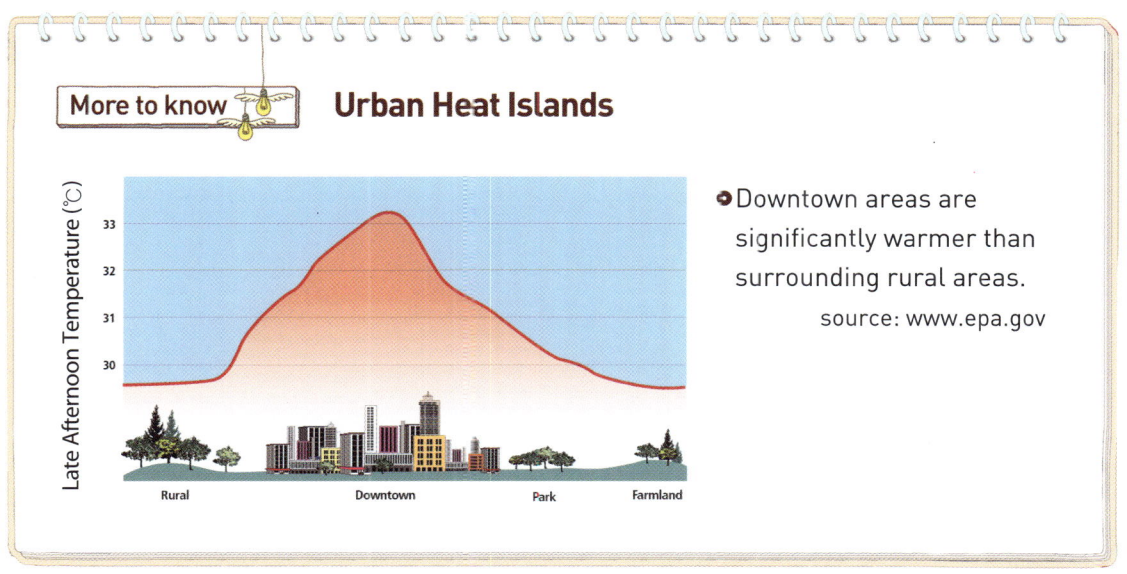

Environment • 21

Reading Helper

A. It...take...for...to (Duration)

> **Examples from the passage**
> • **It** can **take** thousands of years **for** a glacier **to** move a few meters. (Glaciers, Line 5)

Fill in the blanks with the appropriate words.

1 It can _____ several months _____ some children _____ learn the process completely.

2 It will _____ many hours _____ the building _____ cool down after fire.

Complete the sentences using the words given.

3 It took (get prepared / time / the / to / group / for).

→ It took _____

4 (feel comfortable / people / for / to / takes / it / a long time) with change.

→ _____ with change.

B. to (Purpose)

Examples from the passage
- **To** save the forests, we must stop removing trees.   (Tree Removal, Line 11)
= We must stop removing trees **in order to** save the forests.

Fill in the blanks with the appropriate expressions.

- to solve the problems
- to stay healthy
- to meet a friend

1 _____, we should exercise regularly.

2 More ideas are needed _____.

Rewrite the sentences using *in order to*.

3 To succeed, one must have pass on.
→ _____

4 Many volunteers are needed to make the program successful.
→ _____

UNIT 02
History

•• Search! Search!

Find out about the topics using the Internet.
Pharaohs, Ancient Egyptian Burial, The Vikings, Water Clocks

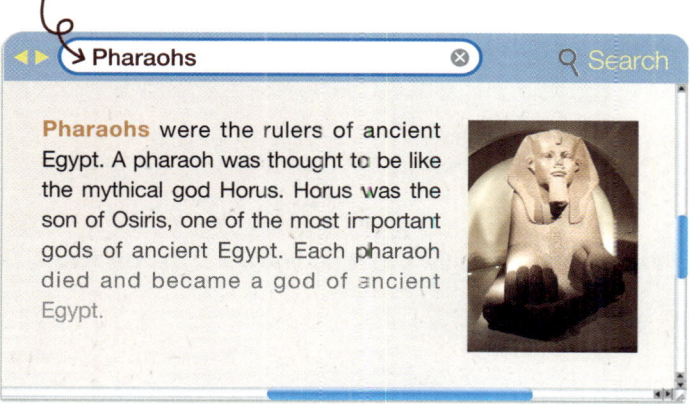

•• Target iBT TOEFL Questions

Finding True Information Questions

- According to paragraph X, which of the following is true of …?
- According to paragraph X, A did B because …
- According to paragraph X, A is(are) …

Finding False Information Questions

- According to paragraph X, which of the following is NOT true of …?
- All of the following are mentioned EXCEPT…

Practice 1

Warm Up

1 Go through the passage quickly to find these words. Use what you know about these words to guess the topic.

> • Ancient Egyptians • burial customs • mummification • tomb

2 Identify the topic and read the passage quickly. What do you think the passage is about?

- Ancient Egyptians' belief in afterlife ○
- Ancient Egyptians' burial customs ○

Read the Passage

Your time (1st): ___ min, (2nd): ___ min

Ancient Egyptian Burial

Ancient Egyptians were very religious. They thought they would live again after death. Their burial customs included making mummies. Mummification is a way of preserving a dead body. First, all of the body's organs are removed, except for the heart. The organs were kept in special jars. After removing the organs, the body was dried with salt. Later, the dried body was wrapped in white fabric. This mummification process takes up to 70 days to finish.

Mummification was common. However, there were different traditions according to social status. Egyptian kings were buried in pyramids. Pyramids are huge triangular structures. They are built of brick or stone.

Other wealthy people were often mummified and buried in mastabas. A mastaba is a rectangular stone tomb. It has a prayer room above ground and a mummified body below ground. Usually, bodies were buried with food and luxury items. Egyptians thought the dead would use them in the afterlife. The graves of some workers contained a mummified body with food and furniture. Other common people were often just wrapped in cloth and buried in the desert sand. Their bodies were also buried with food and everyday objects.

Target iBT TOEFL Questions

1 According to paragraph 1, which of the following is true of mummification?
   Ⓐ After death, all the body's organs are removed.
   Ⓑ It takes more than two months.
   Ⓒ Before the body was dried, it was wrapped in fabric.

2 Which of the following is NOT true of pyramids?
   Ⓐ They are tombs for Egyptian kings.
   Ⓑ They are built with bricks and stones.
   Ⓒ They have a room for prayer above ground.

3 According to paragraph 3, mastabas are
   Ⓐ prayer rooms   Ⓑ tombs for wealthy people   Ⓒ jars for body organs

4 Ancient Egyptians buried food, jewelry and other objects with a dead body because
   Ⓐ they believed there was an afterlife
   Ⓑ they were gifts to the gods
   Ⓒ they didn't want the person's things to be stolen

iBT TOEFL Vocabulary

Fill in the blanks with the appropriate words.

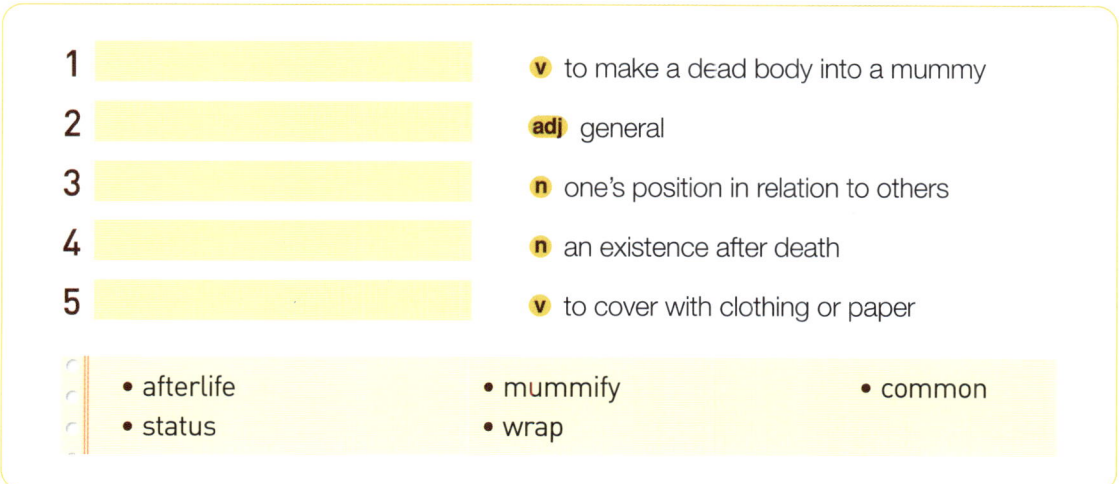

1 _____ v to make a dead body into a mummy
2 _____ adj general
3 _____ n one's position in relation to others
4 _____ n an existence after death
5 _____ v to cover with clothing or paper

• afterlife   • mummify   • common
• status   • wrap

History •• 27

Wrap Up

A Complete the sentences with the appropriate words.

- common
- afterlife
- mummified
- status
- wrapped

1 Ancient Egyptians _____ animals as well as humans.

2 The social _____ of women has changed a great deal.

3 Many of the _____ people were farmers.

4 Ancient Egyptians' burial customs are based on their belief in a(n) _____

5 The mummies were _____ in cloth.

B Number the sentences in the correct order to complete the summary of the passage <Ancient Egyptian Burial>.

____ Then, they dried the body with salts. 1 Ancient Egyptians believed in life after death. ____ First, they removed the body organs of the dead body, except for the heart. ____ Later, the dried body was wrapped in white fabric. 6 The process took more than two months to finish. ____ They preserved the dead body through mummification.

However, the burial customs were different according to social status. Kings were buried in pyramids after mummification. Rich people were mummified and buried in stone tombs with luxury items. On the other hand, common people were buried in the desert sand with everyday objects.

Practice 2

Warm Up

1 What comes to your mind when you think of Egypt? Write a few words.

Read the Passage

Your time (1ˢᵗ): ____ min, (2ⁿᵈ): ____ min

Pharaohs

Pharaohs were the rulers of ancient Egypt. A pharaoh was thought to be like the mythical god Horus. Horus was the son of Osiris, one of the most important gods of ancient Egypt. Each pharaoh died and became a god of ancient Egypt.

Pharaohs were also the political leaders of Egypt. In addition, a pharaoh also <u>owned</u> all the land of Egypt and made the laws. He collected taxes from the people of Egypt. In return, he protected the people and country from attack.

One of the most famous leaders of Egypt was Queen Cleopatra. She is famous for her impact on powerful men. As a woman, Cleopatra could not be a pharaoh. Her younger brother, Ptolemy XIII, was the named pharaoh of her time. She married her brother, the pharaoh, so that she could rule Egypt. She also used leaders of Rome like Emperor Julius Caesar and General Marc Antony to protect her kingdom. She was the true power behind these great men in history.

* own: to have, to possess

Target iBT TOEFL Questions

1 According to the passage, which of the following is true of pharaohs?

Ⓐ They were the sons of the most important god in ancient Egypt.
Ⓑ Both kings and queens could become a pharaoh.
Ⓒ They made the laws of ancient Egypt.

2 According to paragraph 3, Cleopatra married her brother because

Ⓐ she wanted to become a pharaoh
Ⓑ she wanted to rule Egypt
Ⓒ she wanted to protect her brother

3 The word `collected` in the passage is closest in meaning to

Ⓐ asked   Ⓑ gathered   Ⓒ stored

4 The word `impact` in the passage is closest in meaning to

Ⓐ strength   Ⓑ action   Ⓒ influence

iBT TOEFL Vocabulary

Fill in the blanks with the appropriate words.

#		
1	**v**	to keep safe, to guard
2	**n**	an act of trying to destroy
3	**adj**	having great power or force
4	**v**	to control, to direct
5	**n**	an officer of the highest rank in the army

- general
- powerful
- protect
- attack
- rule

Wrap Up

A Complete the sentences with the appropriate words.

- general
- powerful
- protect
- attack
- ruled

1 It is important to keep the country safe from _____.

2 _____ countries control the world through money.

3 Paper recycling can _____ the environment.

4 The _____ was proud of his soldiers.

5 The country was _____ by the military at that time.

B Complete the summary note of the passage <Pharaohs>.

Paragraph 1: About pharaohs
- Pharaohs = r_____ of ancient Egypt

Paragraph 2: The roles of pharaohs
(1) political leaders (2) l_____ owners (3) l_____ makers

Paragraph 3: About Queen Cleopatra
- famous for her i_____ on powerful men
- a w_____ could not be a pharaoh
  → thus she married her b_____ in order to rule Egypt

Test 1

The Vikings

Vikings were pirates from Scandinavia. Scandinavia is the part of Europe that includes Norway, Sweden and Denmark. Vikings are also called "the Norse". They began as great shipbuilders and sailors. Vikings are Norse sailors who attacked England from the 8th century to the 10th century. The Vikings ruled various parts of the British Isles between 793 AD and 1468 AD. The British Isles include England, Scotland, Ireland and Wales.

The Vikings also traveled to many other lands. They were brave explorers of the world. They went as far east as Central Asia. They also went as far west as North America. A Viking man, Bjarni Herjolfsson, discovered America by accident. Strong winds blew his ship off course on the way to Greenland. The year was 985 AD. A few years later, in 1001, Leif Eriksson sailed there to take a good look at it. He was the first European to land in America.

The Vikings' impact on English culture can still be seen today. Many English words, such as "husband", "egg", "law", "knife" and "window", come from Old Norse, the Vikings' language. Even some days of the week are named after Norse gods. Thor was an important Norse god. Every "Thursday" is really "Thor's Day".

* **pirate:** someone who robs at sea

1 According to paragraph 1, which of the following is NOT true of Vikings?

Ⓐ They are also called "the Norse."
Ⓑ They were originally shipbuilders and sailors.
Ⓒ Norse sailors attacked them from the 8th to 10th century.
Ⓓ They ruled many parts of the British Isles.

2 The word it in the passage refers to

Ⓐ America Ⓑ ship Ⓒ Greenland Ⓓ European

3 The word land in the passage is closest in meaning to

Ⓐ find Ⓑ arrive Ⓒ explore Ⓓ live

4 According to paragraph 2, Leif Eriksson was

Ⓐ a traveler who went to Central Asia
Ⓑ an explorer who found America accidentally
Ⓒ a fisherman who went to Greenland in 985 AD
Ⓓ a European who landed in America for the first time

5 According to paragraph 2, Leif Eriksson went to America in 1001 in order to

Ⓐ live there
Ⓑ find treasure
Ⓒ explore a new continent
Ⓓ attack the continent

6 In paragraph 3, the author mentions English words in order to

Ⓐ show the Vikings' impact on English culture
Ⓑ show the Vikings' impact on Europe
Ⓒ show how old the English language is
Ⓓ show that the names of weekdays are really the names of Norse gods

---

More to know — **The Vikings' Impact on English**

- The Vikings brought many old Norse words to the English language. The words are:
    sky, egg, cake, skin, husband, fellow, leg, window,
    skill, ugly, get, give, take, raise, call, die, anger, flat, odd

- The personal pronouns *they*, *their*, and *them* also came from old Norse words.

History • 33

Test 2

Water Clocks

Water clocks are tools for measuring time with water. This method is one of the oldest ways of measuring time. Water clocks were used as early as 4000 BC in China. The oldest water clock is from Egypt. This clock dates back to 1417 - 1379 BC. Water clocks were used in northern Africa until the 20th century. They were also used in India, Greece and Korea.

Water clocks allow a steady amount of water into, or out of, a container. This is how they measure time. In the past, some water clocks used a simple bowl with a small hole in the bottom. The bowl was placed in a larger container of water. As the bowl filled, the time was measured. Other water clocks used a container full of water with a small hole. As the water dripped out, it was caught in another container. Time was measured by markings on one of the containers.

In Greek and Roman times, water clocks were used to measure time for speeches. They were also used in the courts of law. Water clocks in Greece were highly developed. They used more complicated systems. They were also very accurate. Even so, these water clocks always had to be watched by a person known as a timekeeper. Korea was the first country to make an automatic water clock. In 1434, one of the government officials made the first self-timing clock.

1 According to paragraph 1, the oldest water clock is from

Ⓐ China   Ⓑ Egypt   Ⓒ Greece   Ⓓ Korea

2 The word steady in the passage is closest in meaning to

Ⓐ small   Ⓑ regular   Ⓒ safe   Ⓓ total

3 The word it in the passage refers to

Ⓐ container　　Ⓑ hole　　Ⓒ water　　Ⓓ time

4 Using water clocks, time can be measured by

Ⓐ the size of containers
Ⓑ the number of holes in the containers
Ⓒ the amount of water in the containers
Ⓓ the size of holes in the containers

5 The word accurate in the passage is closest in meaning to

Ⓐ correct　　Ⓑ powerful　　Ⓒ perfect　　Ⓓ impressive

6 According to the passage, all of the following countries are mentioned for their use of water clocks EXCEPT

Ⓐ India　　Ⓑ China　　Ⓒ Greece　　Ⓓ Japan

7 According to paragraph 3, which of the following is true of water clocks?

Ⓐ There was no timekeeper for water clocks in Greece.
Ⓑ Water clocks in Greece used complicated systems.
Ⓒ One of the kings invented an automatic water clock in Korea.
Ⓓ They were usually used for measuring time after dark.

Sun Clocks

A sun clock is the oldest type of clock. Sun clocks were first used around 6,000 years ago. They use the sun to tell the time. The shadow of the sun points to a number on a circular board showing the hours. Since sun clocks depend on the sun, they can only be used during the day.

Reading Helper

A. one of the most

Examples from the passage

- Horus was the son of Osiris, **one of the most important gods** of ancient Egypt.
  (Pharaohs, Line 2)
- **One of the most famous leaders** of Egypt was Queen Cleopatra.
  (Pharaohs, Line 7)
- This method is **one of the oldest ways** of measuring time.
  (Water Clocks, Line 1)

Correct the mistakes in the following sentences.

1 Global warming is one of the most serious problem in our society.
→

2 Mother Teresa is one of the most greatest leaders of the 20th century.
→

3 Water is one of the more important natural resources that people need.
→

B. so that (Purpose)

Examples from the passage

- She married her brother, the pharaoh, **so that** she could rule Egypt.

(Pharaohs, Line 10)

Choose the appropriate sentence for each blank.

- Some animals go into a deep sleep over the winter.
- Some animals leave their smell on plants.
- Some fish are colored.

1 _____ so that other animals can recognize them.

2 _____ so that they can survive the cold weather.

3 _____ so that they can hide from their enemies.

UNIT 03
Biology

•• Search! Search!

Find out about the topics using the Internet.
Color Changes, Animals in Danger, Feathers, Hibernation

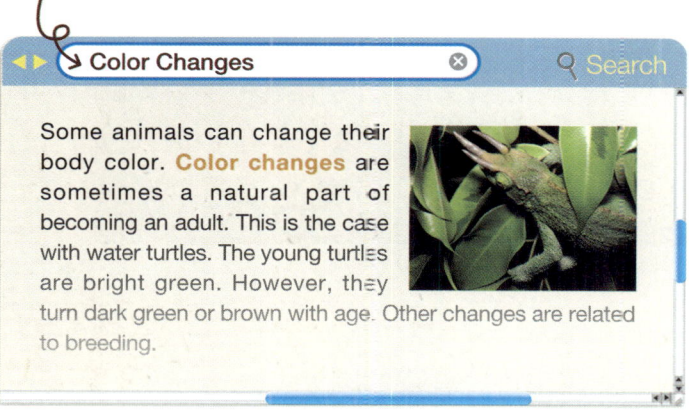

Color Changes

Some animals can change their body color. **Color changes** are sometimes a natural part of becoming an adult. This is the case with water turtles. The young turtles are bright green. However, they turn dark green or brown with age. Other changes are related to breeding.

•• Target iBT TOEFL Questions

Sentence Simplification Questions

Which of the following best expresses the essential information in the highlighted sentence in the passage? Incorrect choices change the meaning in important ways or leave out essential information.

A sentence

Practice 1

Warm Up

1. What kinds of animals change their body colors?

2. Do you know why some animals change their body colors?

Read the Passage

Your time (1st): _____ min, (2nd): _____ min

Color Changes

Some animals can change their body color. Color changes are sometimes a natural part of becoming an adult. This is the case with water turtles. The young turtles are bright green. However, they turn dark green or brown with age. Other changes are related to breeding. Some birds grow more colorful feathers to attract a partner for breeding. Furthermore, the color of some animals changes with the seasonal color changes of the environment. In places where snow falls in winter, many animals turn white as winter comes.

Color changes in mammals and birds occur through molting. Molting is the process through which the color of the hair, skin or feathers becomes a different color. Quick color changes in mammals and birds are unusual because of their fur and feathers. However, some species of animals that have bare facial skin are able to blush. Good examples of this are turkeys and humans. Humans blush because of strong emotions like anger or embarrassment. On the other hand, people can suddenly turn white when they are shocked or afraid. This effect is called blanching.

Target iBT TOEFL Questions

1 Which of the following best expresses the essential information in the highlighted sentence in the passage? Incorrect choices change the meaning in important ways or leave out essential information.

> In places where snow falls in winter, many animals turn white as winter comes.

Ⓐ Some animals change to white close to winter snow seasons.

Ⓑ In snowy places, animals usually look white.

Ⓒ White animals often live in places where snow falls in winter.

2 Which of the following best expresses the essential information in the highlighted sentence in the passage? Incorrect choices change the meaning in important ways or leave out essential information.

> Quick color changes in mammals and birds are unusual because of their fur and feathers.

Ⓐ Fur and feathers cause quick color changes.

Ⓑ Due to fur and feathers, it is uncommon for mammals and birds to change colors quickly.

Ⓒ Due to fur and feathers, color changes in mammals and birds occur suddenly.

iBT TOEFL Vocabulary

Fill in the blanks with the appropriate words.

#		
1	_____	**n** a grown animal or person
2	_____	**v** to arouse the attention of
3	_____	**v** to happen
4	_____	**v** to change the nature, or appearance of
5	_____	**n** any of the feelings including joy, fear, hate
6	_____	**adv** happening quickly

- suddenly
- emotion
- adult
- occur
- attract
- turn

Biology •• 41

Wrap Up

A Find the synonyms for the underlined words.

- adult
- turn
- attract
- emotions
- occurred
- suddenly

1 Talking about <u>feelings</u> can help a person feel better.

2 A child becomes a(n) <u>grown-up</u> by learning social values.

3 Leaves <u>become</u> red or yellow in autumn.

4 The earthquake <u>happened</u> in the morning on Friday.

5 The virus <u>unexpectedly</u> appeared in humans.

6 Some birds use sound to <u>charm</u> their mates.

B Complete the summary note of the passage <Color Changes>.

- Some animals change their body colors when
    (1) they become a_____
       e.g. water t_____ (bright green → dark green or brown)
    (2) they a_____ their mates
       e.g. some birds grow more colorful feathers
    (3) the s_____ changes
       e.g. some animals turn w_____ as winter comes
- Color changes in mammals and birds occur through m_____.
- Animals with bare facial skin blush and b_____.

Practice 2

Warm Up

1 Go through the passage quickly to find these words. Use what you know about these words to guess the topic.

- extinct
- pollution
- destruction
- overhunting

2 Identify the topic and read the passage quickly. What do you think the passage is mainly about?

- Why dinosaurs disappeared ○
- Why animals become extinct ○

Read the Passage

Your time (1st): _____ min, (2nd): _____ min

Animals in Danger

Some animals are in danger of becoming extinct. The dinosaur is a famous example of an extinct animal. Animals disappear for many reasons. Dinosaurs became extinct because of major climate changes. Today, extinction is mainly caused by human beings.

The development of industry and farming threatens over a thousand species around the world. Pollution caused by cars, garbage and factories is a danger to many types of plants and animals. Another danger is the destruction of a species' natural environment. Humans cut and burn many types of forests for wood and farmland. This kills the plants, the trees, and also the animals in the area.

Humans have also introduced new species to certain areas. This has threatened many native species that live and grow naturally in these places. When a species that is not native is brought to an area by humans, the natural balance of life is changed. Native species may become threatened by this change. Humans can also change this natural balance by overhunting. Many species are now in danger because people have killed so many animals in a short period of time. Some people say humans are the world's most dangerous hunters.

Target iBT TOEFL Questions

1 Which of the following best expresses the essential information in the highlighted sentence in the passage? Incorrect choices change the meaning in important ways or leave out essential information.

> The development of industry and farming threatens over a thousand species around the world.

Ⓐ Industry and farming scare some species of plants and animals.
Ⓑ Growing industry and farming may kill species of plants and animals.
Ⓒ Growing industry and farming is developing species.

2 Which of the following best expresses the essential information in the highlighted sentence in the passage? Incorrect choices change the meaning in important ways or leave out essential information.

> When a species that is not native is brought to an area by humans, the natural balance of life is changed.

Ⓐ New animals introduced by humans destroy the balance of life.
Ⓑ Humans and species change the balance of life.
Ⓒ The natural balance can be changed by new species introduced by humans.

iBT TOEFL Vocabulary

Fill in the blanks with the appropriate words.

1. _____ **v** to make a threat against someone
2. _____ **adj** no longer existing
3. _____ **n** the process or result of developing
4. _____ **n** the act of destroying
5. _____ **n** the introduction of harmful substances into the environment

• extinct   • development   • threaten   • pollution   • destruction

Wrap Up

A Complete the sentences with the appropriate words.

- extinct
- threatens
- pollution
- development
- destruction

1 Polar bears are likely to become _____ by 2050.

2 Cars, buses, and airplanes may cause air _____ .

3 The results give clues about the _____ of human language.

4 The recent forest fires have caused widespread _____ .

5 Climate change _____ the Arctic.

B Complete the summary note of the passage <Animals in Danger>.

- Many species are in danger of becoming extinct.
- Reasons: 1. c_____ change
  2. the development of industry and farming
  3. p_____
  4. destruction of their natural environment
  5. the introduction of new s_____
  6. o_____

Feathers

The feather is a unique feature of birds. Only birds have feathers. In other words, everything with feathers is a bird. Feathers come in many shapes, sizes and colors. They differ depending on the needs of the bird. Feathers have many important purposes in helping birds survive. These purposes include temperature control and flight.

Scientists believe that feathers first developed for protection from extreme temperatures. Feathers keep birds cool in hot weather or warm in cold weather. [■A] When it is cold outside, birds will fluff out their feathers. [■B] When a bird's feathers are fluffed out, there is a space full of warm air between its skin and the cold outside air. [■C] When the outside air is hot, a bird flattens its feathers close to its skin. [■D]

The ability to fly developed because of birds' feathers. Over time, feathers became stronger, lighter and larger. As a result, flight became easier. Flight allows birds to escape from danger. It also helps them to find food. Different birds developed different types of feathers for their specific needs. For example, an owl's feathers have fluffy tips instead of round tips like most birds. This allows owls to fly more quietly. It also helps them to hunt small animals for food.

1 The word feature in the passage is closest in meaning to

  Ⓐ quality   Ⓑ type   Ⓒ behavior   Ⓓ characteristic

2 Which of the following best expresses the essential information in the highlighted sentence in the passage? Incorrect choices change the meaning in important ways or leave out essential information.

Feathers have many important purposes in helping birds survive.

  Ⓐ Feathers survive for important reasons.   Ⓑ Birds survive because of feathers.
  Ⓒ Feathers do many things to help birds survive.   Ⓓ Feathers are important for birds.

3. Look at the four squares [■] that indicate where the following sentence could be added to the passage.

   This stops the hot outside air from reaching the bird's skin so it stays cool.

   Where would the sentence best fit?

4. Which of the following best expresses the essential information in the highlighted sentence in the passage? Incorrect choices change the meaning in important ways or leave out essential information.

   The ability to fly developed because of birds' feathers.

   Ⓐ Feathers grew so birds could fly.
   Ⓑ Birds began to fly after feathers developed.
   Ⓒ Feathers help birds fly.
   Ⓓ Birds could not fly without wings.

5. According to paragraph 3, what can be inferred about bird feathers?
   Ⓐ They all have the same qualities.
   Ⓑ They are mostly used for flying.
   Ⓒ They became smaller.
   Ⓓ They have evolved over time.

6. The author mentions owl's feathers in order to
   Ⓐ show that all bird feathers are similar
   Ⓑ give an example of special feathers for special purposes
   Ⓒ show how feathers have become stronger, lighter and larger
   Ⓓ give an example of lighter feathers

 **Feather Functions**

- **Flight**: Feathers play an important role in flight.
- **Mating**: Male birds' feathers are usually more colorful than the feathers of the female. The feathers of the male can have an impact on how attractive he is to a female.
- **Keeping body temperature**: Feathers keep birds warm.

Biology •• 47

Test 2

Hibernation

Some animals fall into a long sleep in the winter. This type of sleep is called hibernation. Hibernation is one way that animals adapt to cold weather. Animals eat much more food in the autumn to prepare for hibernation. They store extra fat to use for energy during their long sleep. During hibernation, the animals breathe slowly. Their heartbeats also slow down. In this way, they use much less energy. As their bodily activity slows in the fall, animals become less able to move. They slowly fall into a type of sleep.

One type of hibernation happens in short periods. It lasts from a few days to a few weeks. The length of the period depends on the animal, its size, the temperature and the season. These times of inactivity are interrupted by brief periods of activity. When active, the animal's body temperature rises to a normal level. For example, skunks may "sleep" for up to 100 days at a time. They awaken to find food, then they go back to sleep.

Hibernation helps animals survive difficult weather conditions. However, animals can still freeze or die while hibernating. Less ability to move also makes it easier for other animals to attack them. Thus, for protection, many animals hibernate in safe areas like caves or underground spaces. These places often stay above freezing even when the outside temperature is much colder.

1 According to paragraph 1, animals hibernate in order to

Ⓐ eat less food
Ⓑ protect themselves from enemies
Ⓒ use less energy in cold weather
Ⓓ find a safe area to sleep

2 Which of the following best expresses the essential information in the highlighted sentence in the passage? Incorrect choices change the meaning in important ways or leave out essential information.

They store extra fat to use for energy during their long sleep.

Ⓐ They build up some fat so that they can use it for energy during hibernation.
Ⓑ They use fat as their energy source.
Ⓒ They gather some foods to eat later while hibernating.
Ⓓ Fat is used for energy for some animals during the period of winter sleep.

3 Which of the following best expresses the essential information in the highlighted sentence in the passage? Incorrect choices change the meaning in important ways or leave out essential information.

As their bodily activity slows in the fall, animals become less able to move.

Ⓐ Hibernation makes animals move slowly in the fall.
Ⓑ Hibernating animals have heavy bodies.
Ⓒ Hibernating animals are able to move fast in the fall.
Ⓓ Animals' bodies become less active before hibernation begins.

4 The word interrupted in the passage is closest in meaning to

Ⓐ changed　　　Ⓑ broken　　　Ⓒ damaged　　　Ⓓ made

5 According to paragraph 3, many animals hibernate in caves or underground spots because

Ⓐ it is quiet there　　　　　　　　Ⓑ it is safer and warmer there
Ⓒ it is dark there　　　　　　　　Ⓓ other animals will also sleep there

6 According to the passage, what can be inferred about hibernation?

Ⓐ Hibernation can also help animals survive during the hot summer.
Ⓑ Hibernation is useful but not perfect for survival.
Ⓒ Hibernation makes animals freeze in cold weather.
Ⓓ Hibernation is a way of avoiding enemies.

 **Estivation**

Estivation is another form of "sleep." It is the period when an animal is inactive because of heat and/or drought. Some examples of estivators include: bees, snakes, lizards, and snails.

Reading Helper

A. However

Examples from the passage

- The young turtles are bright green. **However**, they turn dark green or brown with age.
  (Color Changes, Line 2)

- Hibernation helps animals survive difficult weather conditions. **However**, animals can still freeze or die while hibernating.
  (Hibernation, Line 14)

B. As a result

Examples from the passage

- Over time, feathers became stronger, lighter and larger. **As a result**, flight became easier.
  (Feathers, Line 12)

C. Furthermore

Examples from the passage

- Some birds grow more colorful feathers to attract a partner for breeding. **Furthermore**, the color of some animals changes with the seasonal color changes of the environment.
  (Color Changes, Line 4)

D. On the other hand

Examples from the passage

- Humans blush because of strong emotions like anger or embarrassment. **On the other hand**, people can suddenly turn white when they are shocked or afraid.

(Color Changes, Line 12)

E. In other words

Examples from the passage

- Only birds have feathers. **In other words**, everything with feathers is a bird.

(Feathers, Line 1)

Go through the four passages in Unit 3 and find these expressions;

for example, thus

UNIT 04
Anthropology

•• Search! Search!

Find out about the topics using the Internet.
The Maya, Shamans, Totem Poles, The Inuit

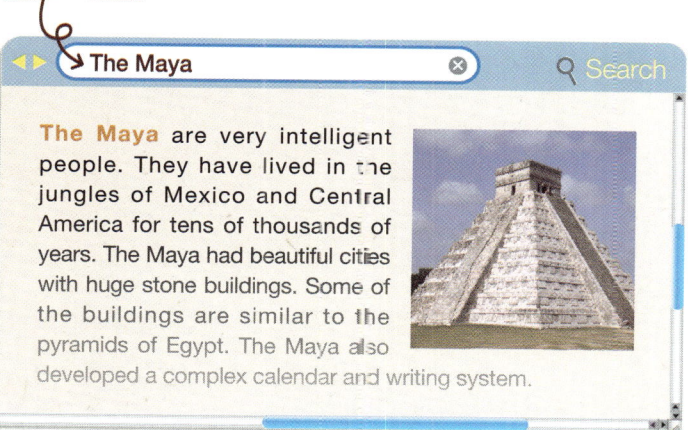

The Maya are very intelligent people. They have lived in the jungles of Mexico and Central America for tens of thousands of years. The Maya had beautiful cities with huge stone buildings. Some of the buildings are similar to the pyramids of Egypt. The Maya also developed a complex calendar and writing system.

•• Target iBT TOEFL Questions

Inference Questions

- According to paragraph X, what can be inferred about _____?

- According to paragraph X, it can be inferred about _____ that...

Practice 1

Warm Up

1 Go through the passage quickly to find these words. Use what you know about these words to guess the topic.

- Maya
- disappear
- society
- mysterious
- collapsed

2 Identify the topic and read the passage quickly. What do you think the passage is about?

○ The end of ancient Mayan cities   ○ Saving the Mayan culture

Read the Passage

Your time (1st): ____ min, (2nd): ____ min

The Maya

The Maya are very intelligent people. They have lived in the jungles of Mexico and Central America for tens of thousands of years. The Maya had beautiful cities with huge stone buildings. Some of the buildings are similar to the pyramids of Egypt. The Maya also developed a complex calendar and writing system.

Mayan society has existed for more than thirty thousand years. However, their cities were collapsed. The reason is not really known. Some people say that the common people or slaves fought back against the upper class. These people believe that the society could not survive without the help of the working people. Others think that poor farming methods were the reason. The overuse of trees and land made growing good food difficult. Some scientists study Mayan bones. They think poor nutrition may have ended Mayan society. Others suggest disease and climate change caused the Maya to disappear into jungles. Whatever the true reason for their mysterious disappearance, the Maya left behind many amazing objects.

Target iBT TOEFL Questions

1. According to paragraph 1, it can be inferred that

    Ⓐ the Maya visited Egyptian buildings
    Ⓑ Mayan civilization was fairly well developed
    Ⓒ the Maya recorded their history

2. According to paragraph 2, what can be inferred about the Maya?

    Ⓐ All of them were farmers.
    Ⓑ There were different social classes.
    Ⓒ The Maya influenced Egypt.

iBT TOEFL Vocabulary

Fill in the blanks with the appropriate words.

1	_____	**v** to be present, to live
2	_____	**v** to grow into a more advanced state
3	_____	**adj** smart, clever
4	_____	**n** a system that shows the length of the year
5	_____	**n** an explanation for some phenomenon

- develop
- intelligent
- exist
- reason
- calendar

Anthropology •• 55

Wrap Up

A Complete the sentences with the appropriate words.

- developed
- intelligent
- calendar
- reason
- existed

1. _____ students tend to learn faster.

2. The temple has _____ since 1898.

3. The southern part of the country has _____ the most.

4. Mayans developed a _____ of 360 days.

5. The true _____ for the failure is not known.

B Complete the summary of the passage <The Maya>.

The Maya have lived in Mexico and Central A_____ since ancient times. They had a very d_____ culture for that time. They once had beautiful cities with s_____ buildings. They also developed a calendar and a complex type of writing. However, their cities were c_____. The reasons for their disappearance are not really known yet. So far, slaves' anger against the u_____ class, lack of food, d_____ and climate change are some suspected reasons.

Practice 2

Warm Up

A Shaman

A Shaman's Drum

1 Have you ever heard about "Shamans"?

2 Do you have "Shamans" in your country?

Read the Passage

Your time (1st): ____ min, (2nd): ____ min

Shamans

A shaman is a person with special abilities. He or she can talk with spirits. Shamans connect humans to spirits. Shamans do many jobs in a village. They help sick people. Shamans also help stop fights between people. Most of all, they give help in decision making. People ask them for advice about hunting, war, marriage, death, childbirth, and farming. The shaman talks with spirits to get information about these decisions. To communicate with spirits, a shaman usually enters a trance. A trance is a special state of mind. Shamans use many methods to enter a trance. For example, they can play drums, dance or smoke dried herbs and flowers. Some shamans do not eat for many days to go into a trance.

The tradition of shamans came from Northern Asia thousands of years ago. The tradition can be found all over the world, from Siberia to North America. In many countries, shamans still have an important role in modern life.

Target iBT TOEFL Questions

1 According to the passage, what can be inferred about shamans?

Ⓐ They no longer exist.
Ⓑ They were leaders of a village.
Ⓒ They are important in people's lives.

2 The word them in the passage refers to

Ⓐ humans   Ⓑ spirits   Ⓒ shamans

3 Which of the following is NOT mentioned as a method of getting into a trance?

Ⓐ eating flowers   Ⓑ drumming   Ⓒ dancing

iBT TOEFL Vocabulary

Fill in the blanks with the appropriate words.

#		
1		n power to do something or a special skill
2		n a supernatural being or soul
3		n an opinion offered as a guide
4		n the act of making up one's mind
5		n a continuing pattern of beliefs and customs in a society
6		n function

- tradition
- advice
- role
- decision
- ability
- spirit

Wrap Up

A Choose the correct words from the box to change the words in bold.

- abilities
- decisions
- advice
- spirits
- traditions
- role

1 Some animals have natural **traditions** to change their body colors.

2 They finally made **spirits** after much thought.

3 It is better to ask for **abilities** before making an important decision.

4 Different countries have different holiday **role**.

5 The people who can communicate with **decisions** are called shamans.

6 The school plays an important **advice** in the community.

B Complete the summary of the passage <Shamans>.

s_____ are people who can talk with the spirit world. They play many important roles in a v_____. They help sick people. They also help people make good d_____. They use many methods to get in touch with spirits, such as drumming, d_____ and smoking dried herbs and flowers. Some shamans do not e_____ in order to talk with spirits. They still have an important role in modern life.

Anthropology •• 59

Totem Poles

The Northwest Native Americans were well-known for their totem poles. Totem poles are poles with animal faces. The animal faces are carved into huge trees. The native peoples sometimes paint the totem poles.

A "totem" is a symbol of a Native American family. Each family uses a different animal as its totem. Totem poles are usually located at the entrance of a village. They show which families live in the village.

Totem poles are also made to tell stories. Some of the stories are about the family who had the pole made. They are also used to honor deceased elders and important events. Other poles tell Native American legends. These legends often use animals to symbolize people and events in the family's history.

In modern times, totem poles have become a unique symbol of Northwestern Native culture and history. Indeed, they are beautiful pieces of art. They are also viewed as a strong symbol of Native American pride.

* **honor:** to show respect towards

---

1 The word its in the passage refers to

Ⓐ symbol   Ⓑ family   Ⓒ animal   Ⓓ village

2 The word deceased in the passage is closest in meaning to

Ⓐ respectful   Ⓑ important   Ⓒ great   Ⓓ dead

3 The word <mark>unique</mark> in the passage is closest in meaning to

    Ⓐ tall   Ⓑ special   Ⓒ lucky   Ⓓ traditional

4 All of the followings are mentioned in the passage EXCEPT

    Ⓐ Totem poles represent families
    Ⓑ Totem poles tell stories and legends
    Ⓒ Native Americans have stories with animals in totem poles
    Ⓓ Totem poles could be used for direction

5 According to the passage, it can be inferred that

    Ⓐ totem poles were made for many purposes
    Ⓑ totem poles are no longer made
    Ⓒ Native Americans are hunters
    Ⓓ many museums house totem poles

6 Which of the following is NOT mentioned as a purpose of totem poles?

    Ⓐ They show who lives in a village.
    Ⓑ They are used as entrances.
    Ⓒ They honor important events.
    Ⓓ They represent legends.

More to know   **Animal Characteristics and Meaning**

- **Bee:** organized, industrial, productive, wise
- **Deer:** compassion, peace, intellectual, gentle, caring, kind
- **Dog:** noble, faithful, loyal, protection, guidance
- **Cat:** sensuality, mystery, magic, independence

Test 2

The Inuit

The Inuit are native people who live in the northern Arctic area. The Arctic is the coldest area on Earth. It can get as cold as -46℃ in the winter. Even in the summer, there is almost no plant growth in the area. Living conditions in the Arctic would be very difficult for most people. However, the Inuit have existed well in the Arctic for at least ten thousand years.

Since there are almost no plants in the Arctic, the Inuit eat mostly fish and meat. In the winter, they hunt large animals like seals and polar bears. These creatures provide the Inuit with the necessary fats and nutrients to survive the harsh conditions of the Arctic. The Inuit use every part of their kill. Animals are used to make food, clothes, houses, and boats.

The Inuit are famous for building igloos. An igloo is a round house built from blocks of snow. In fact, the Inuit use igloos on winter hunting trips away from their villages. Permanent Inuit homes are built from rocks, dirt and animal skins. Animal skins are also used to make all the clothing of the Inuit. Inuit clothing is especially suited to staying warm in the cold Arctic climate.

* **provide:** to give   **permanent:** long-lasting

1 According to paragraph 1, it can be inferred about the life of the Inuit that

Ⓐ the Inuit are upset about cold temperatures
Ⓑ the Inuit have adapted to their environment
Ⓒ the Inuit create many things with ice
Ⓓ the Inuit grow plants to live in the Arctic

2 According to paragraph 2, the Inuit hunt large animals in order to

Ⓐ make tools
Ⓑ get necessary fat and nutrients
Ⓒ store food for the winter
Ⓓ make money

3 Which of the following best expresses the essential information in the highlighted sentence in the passage? Incorrect choices change the meaning in important ways or leave out essential information.

> Since there are almost no plants in the Arctic, the Inuit eat mostly fish and meat.

Ⓐ The Inuit couldn't produce enough food.
Ⓑ The Inuit eat fish because it contains many important nutrients they need.
Ⓒ The Inuit always eat fish and meat because it's hard to grow plants in the Arctic.
Ⓓ The Inuit rely on fish and meat for nutrition as there are few plants in the Arctic.

4 The word harsh in the passage is closest in meaning to

Ⓐ current   Ⓑ hard   Ⓒ sharp   Ⓓ general

5 According to paragraph 3, which of the following is true of igloos?

Ⓐ They are shelters on winter hunting trips.
Ⓑ They are built from blocks of stone.
Ⓒ They are permanent homes.
Ⓓ They are sometimes dangerous.

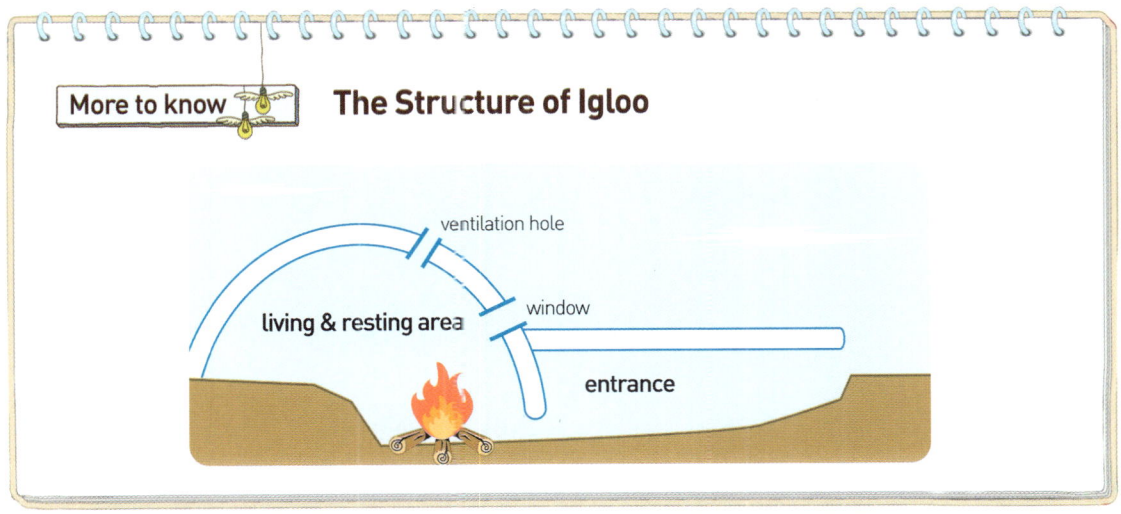

More to know

The Structure of Igloo

Reading Helper

A. since (because)

> **Examples from the passage**
> - **Since** there are almost no plants in the Arctic, the Inuit eat mostly fish and meat.
> (The Inuit, Line 6)
>
> = The Inuit eat mostly fish and meat **since** there are almost no plants in the Arctic.

Combine the two sentences using *since*.

1 Some people do not eat meat. They believe in the rights of animals.

→

2 Ants live in groups. Ants are naturally very social.

→

3 Most tornadoes form suddenly. There is little time for preparation.

→

4 Deserts are dry. Very few plants can grow.

→

B. people think / say / believe that

Examples from the passage

- **Some people say that** the common people or slaves fought back against the upper class. (The Maya, Line 8)

- **These people believe that** the society could not survive without the help of the working people. (The Maya, Line 9)

- **Others think that** poor farming methods were the reason. (The Maya, Line 11)

Complete the sentences using the expressions in bold above.

1. _____ zoos are bad for animals.

2. _____ computers have made life more stressful.

3. _____ they can learn better by themselves.
   _____ it is always better to have a teacher.

UNIT 05
Literature

•• Search! Search!

Find out about the topics using the Internet.
Emily Dickinson, Gulliver's Travels, Detective Novels, Oral Stories in Africa

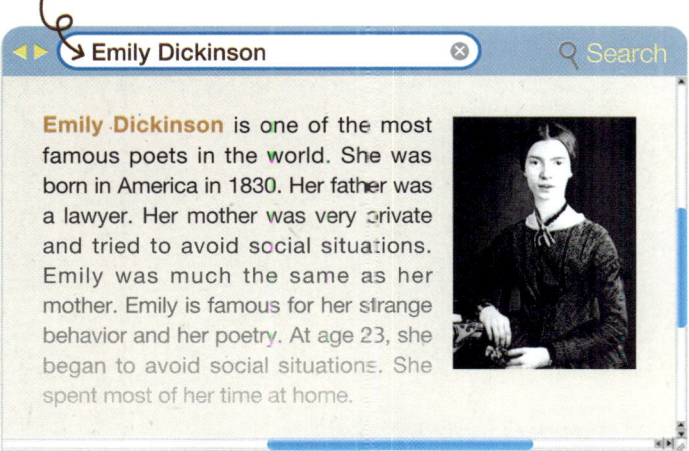

•• Target iBT TOEFL Questions

Rhetorical Purpose Questions

- The author mentions _____ in order to
- The author discusses _____ by (giving examples...)
- What's the function of paragraph X as it relates to the rest of the passage?

Practice 1

Warm Up

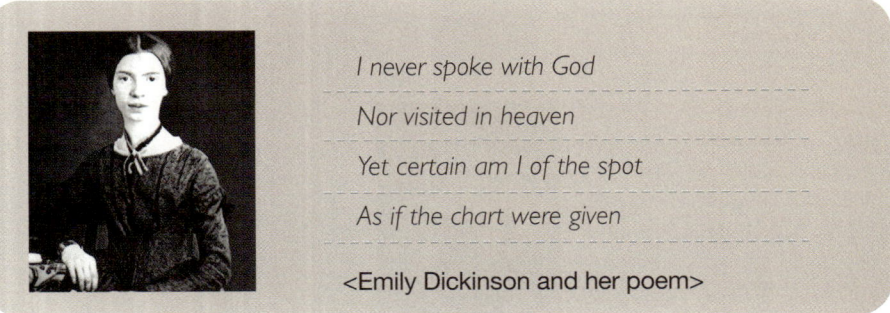

I never spoke with God
Nor visited in heaven
Yet certain am I of the spot
As if the chart were given

<Emily Dickinson and her poem>

1 Have you ever read or written poems?

2 What is your favorite poem? Who is your favorite poet?

Read the Passage

Your time (1st): ____ min, (2nd): ____ min

Emily Dickinson

Emily Dickinson is one of the most famous poets in the world. She was born in America in 1830. Her father was a lawyer. Her mother was very private and tried to avoid social situations.

Emily was much the same as her mother . Emily is famous for her strange behavior and her poetry. At age 23, she began to avoid social situations. She spent most of her time at home. She did not often have visitors. Some people think that failed love changed Emily, but the real reason is not known.

Very few of Emily Dickinson's poems were published when she was alive. When she died in 1886, over a thousand poems were found in her home. Emily made the poems into small books. She had sewn them together by hand. She stored them in a wooden box in her bedroom.

After her death, many of Emily's poems were published. Emily's poetry quickly became famous. Her old school teachers were not surprised. Her poems had impressed her teachers and classmates many years earlier.

Target iBT TOEFL Questions

1. In paragraph 2, the author mentions her mother in order to

   Ⓐ discuss Emily's family history
   Ⓑ explain her mother's character
   Ⓒ show the reason for Emily's character

2. What's the function of paragraph 3 as it relates to the rest of the passage?

   Ⓐ It further shows how private Emily was in her life.
   Ⓑ It shows the quality of her writing.
   Ⓒ It explains her writing style more in detail.

3. In paragraph 4, the author mentions her teachers and classmates in order to

   Ⓐ show Emily's lifetime writing talent
   Ⓑ show Emily's education history
   Ⓒ show how popular Emily was in school

iBT TOEFL Vocabulary

Fill in the blanks with the appropriate words.

#	Word		Definition
1		n	a person who writes poetry
2		adj	personal, individual
3		n	the general state of something
4		v	to keep away from someone or something
5		adj	not far from another
6		v	to have an emotional impact on

- poet
- impress
- close
- private
- avoid
- situation

Literature •• 69

Wrap Up

A Complete the sentences with the appropriate words.

- avoid
- poet
- impressed
- private
- close
- situation

1 A _____ is a person who expresses his/her feelings in beautiful language.

2 Famous people also have the right to have a _____ life.

3 Some people tend to _____ responsibilities at work.

4 The show _____ everyone.

5 _____ friends can be as important as family.

6 The new plan made the bad _____ worse.

B Check (✔) whether the sentences are True (T) or False (F) according to the passage <Emily Dickinson>.

1 Emily Dickinson is a well-known poet.　　T☐　　F☐

2 Emily was born in America in 1930.　　T☐　　F☐

3 Emily spent most of her time at home with her visitors.　　T☐　　F☐

4 Many of her poems were published after she died.　　T☐　　F☐

5 She wrote over a thousand poems.　　T☐　　F☐

Practice 2

Warm Up

1 Go through the passage quickly to find these words. Use what you know about these words to guess the topic.

- African literature
- oral stories
- passed through
- myth
- legend
- folktale
- poems

2 Identify the topic and read the passage quickly. What do you think the passage is about?

- African history ○
- African literature ○

Read the Passage

Your time (1st): ____ min, (2nd): ____ min

Oral Stories in Africa

In African history, the common method of sharing stories was oral. In fact, writing was not often used for stories until the 20th century. Africa's oral tradition has had a profound influence on modern African literature.

Oral stories are passed through many generations for a few reasons. These include recording events, teaching and entertaining. There are many types of oral stories in Africa. Some examples are myths, legends, folktales, and poems.

A myth is a story about the universe, the world, or people. Myths include gods as well as powers of nature. A legend is a story passed through generations that cannot be proven true. Legends often include heroes and monsters. A folktale is a story told for entertainment. It also teaches good behavior. These tales often include people or animals with special abilities. Poems tell a story in a rhythmic or song-like way.

Literature •• 71

Target iBT TOEFL Questions

1 The author mentions writing in paragraph 1 in order to

- Ⓐ emphasize the influence of oral tradition in African literature
- Ⓑ explain why writing began late
- Ⓒ compare speaking and writing

2 What is the function of paragraph 3 as it relates to the rest of the passage?

- Ⓐ It gives several examples of myths in Africa.
- Ⓑ It explains the types of African stories in detail.
- Ⓒ It compares oral storytelling with writing.

iBT TOEFL Vocabulary

Fill in the blanks with the appropriate words.

#	Word		Definition
1	_____	**n**	a way of doing something
2	_____	**adj**	of deep meaning
3	_____	**n**	a group of people born about the same time
4	_____	**adj**	told by mouth, using speech
5	_____	**v**	to show the truth of something with examples

- method
- generation
- oral
- prove
- profound

Wrap Up

A Find the synonyms for the underlined words.

- method
- oral
- profound
- generations
- proved

1 The skills were handed down through <u>ages</u>.

2 Copernicus <u>showed</u> that the Earth goes around the Sun.

3 The Internet has a <u>deep</u> effect on people.

4 The <u>spoken</u> tradition was important in passing on African history.

5 Many researchers used the scientific <u>technique</u> to solve the problems.

B Correct the underlined words in the summary of the passage <Oral Stories in Africa>.

Many stories were told by mouth in <u>American</u> →   history. They were told to record events, to <u>learn</u> →   , and to entertain. There are many types of <u>written</u> →   stories in Africa including myths, legends, folktales, and <u>poets</u> →   .

C Match the word with the correct explanation.

1 legends   Ⓐ explain the universe, the world, and people

2 poems   Ⓑ include heroes and monsters

3 myths   Ⓒ were told for entertainment and to teach good behavior

4 folktales   Ⓓ tell a story in a rhythmic way

Literature •• 73

Test 1

Detective Novels

There were many changes in Europe in the nineteenth century. New machines changed people's lifestyles. Factories were built, and cities were built around them. Later, crime became a problem in cities, and detectives were needed to catch criminals. This excited many writers. They began to write about detectives. Their writings are known as detective novels.

Writers like Francois-Eugene Vidocq wrote about detectives. Vidocq introduced the first detective novel in 1828 in France. The novel was very popular. After him, other French writers began to write about detectives. For example, Victor Hugo wrote *Les Misérables*. In England, Charles Dickens wanted to write crime stories. One of his most famous stories is *Great Expectations*. The American writer Edgar Allan Poe was influenced by Dickens and Vidocq. Poe wrote three famous novels about an unusual detective. But the most famous detective in the world is Sherlock Holmes. In 1887, Sir Arthur Conan Doyle published his first story about Detective Sherlock Holmes and his friend Doctor Watson. More than a hundred years later, his stories continue to entertain readers. They are still interesting and they inspire other stories about great detectives.

1. The word them in the passage refers to

   Ⓐ people   Ⓑ machines   Ⓒ factories   Ⓓ cities

2. According to the passage, detective novels

   Ⓐ were stories about criminals
   Ⓑ became popular in the 20th century
   Ⓒ began after crime caused problems in cities
   Ⓓ began with Sherlock Holmes

3 The word inspire in the passage is closest in meaning to

Ⓐ start　　　Ⓑ compete　　　Ⓒ touch　　　Ⓓ influence

4 In paragraph 2, the author discusses detective novels by

Ⓐ introducing American writers
Ⓑ naming the criminals
Ⓒ listing examples of them
Ⓓ introducing detectives

5 According to paragraph 2, which of the following is NOT true of Sherlock Holmes?

Ⓐ The stories about him are still popular.
Ⓑ He was invented by Sir Arthur Conan Doyle.
Ⓒ He is a very famous detective character in Poe's stories.
Ⓓ The first story about him was published in 1887.

6 What is the function of paragraph 1 as it relates to the rest of the passage?

Ⓐ It shows the reason detective stories appeared.
Ⓑ It gives a general overview of detective novels.
Ⓒ It questions the development of detective novels.
Ⓓ It highlights how police stopped criminals.

| More to know  | **The Work of Charles Dickens: Famous Titles** |

Charles Dickens was born in England in 1812. He is a famous author and poet. He wrote great stories/books, such as

The Adventures of Oliver Twist	1837 - 1839 (Monthly Serial)
A Christmas Carol	1843
Hard Times	1854
Great Expectations	1860 - 1861 (Weekly Serial)

UNIT 5

Literature •• 75

Test 2

Gulliver's Travels

Jonathan Swift wrote the novel, *Gulliver's Travels*. This book is his most noted story. It was published in 1726 when Swift was almost sixty years old. He was a man with strong opinions. He often spoke out against his culture and country. He frequently criticized Britain and Europe in his writing.

At first, *Gulliver's Travels* seems to just be an adventure story about an English sailor. The sailor, Gulliver, travels to many islands. He meets many strange people. Gulliver meets people who are only 15 centimeters tall. He also meets giants. They treat him like he is a pet animal. He even goes to a land with scientists. The scientists studied useless things, including ways to make sunshine with cucumbers. Finally, Gulliver goes to an island where there are horses. These horses are very clever and honorable. On the same island live the "Yahoos." The Yahoos are very rude humans.

If we look closely at *Gulliver's Travels*, we can see Jonathan Swift's real purpose. He used the adventures of Gulliver to comment on problems in real life. His stories are educational as well as entertaining, because they show some dark aspects of modern life.

* criticize: speak against something

1 The word noted in the passage is closest in meaning to

Ⓐ well-known Ⓑ unique Ⓒ important Ⓓ dark

2 The word frequently in the passage is closest in meaning to

Ⓐ mostly Ⓑ suddenly Ⓒ often Ⓓ rarely

3 In paragraph 2, the author explains the story of Gulliver by

  Ⓐ repeating parts of the book
  Ⓑ summarizing characters and events from the story
  Ⓒ listing the characters of the book
  Ⓓ introducing Gulliver's opinions on his journeys

4 The word purpose in the passage is closest in meaning to

  Ⓐ idea Ⓑ goal Ⓒ effect Ⓓ characteristic

5 Which of the following best expresses the essential information in the highlighted sentence in the passage? Incorrect answer choices change the meaning in important ways or leave out essential information.

> He used the adventures of Gulliver to comment on problems in real life.

  Ⓐ Jonathan Swift criticized Gulliver's adventures.
  Ⓑ *Gulliver's Travels* was written to talk about adventure in real life.
  Ⓒ He talked about problems in real life through the adventures of Gulliver.
  Ⓓ Jonathan Swift went on adventures to solve real problems in his life.

6 The word they in the passage refers to

  Ⓐ Yahoos Ⓑ adventures Ⓒ problems Ⓓ stories

7 According to the passage, *Gulliver's Travels* is

  Ⓐ a commentary about modern life
  Ⓑ a story about a giant
  Ⓒ a strange adventure story
  Ⓓ a biographical story

Reading Helper

A. as well as

> **Examples from the passage**
> - Myths include gods **as well as** powers of nature. (Oral Stories in Africa, Line 7)
> - His stories are educational **as well as** entertaining, because they show some dark aspects of modern life. (Gulliver's Travels, Line 15)

Make sentences using the words given in the parenthesis.

1 The feathers (flight, heating, for, as, are, as, well)

→ The feathers _____

2 The student (witty, is, as, intelligent, well, as)

→ The student _____

3 Depression can (affect, as, well, children, as, adults)

→ _____

B. seem to

Examples from the passage
- At first, *Gulliver's Travels* **seems to** just be an adventure story about an English sailor.

(Gulliver's Travels, Line 5)

Rewrite the sentences using the expression *seem to*.

1 The house is old.

→

2 The writer knows what his readers want.

→

3 The search engine has a problem.

→

4 Exercising is the answer to weight loss.

→

UNIT 06
Astronomy

•• Search! Search!

Find out about the topics using the Internet.
Supernovas, Humans in Space, Jupiter, Black Holes

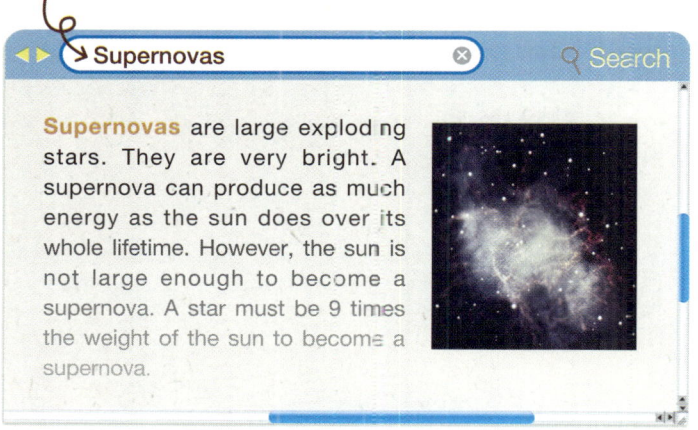

•• Target iBT TOEFL Questions

Insert Text Questions

Look at the four squares [■] that indicate where the following sentence could be added to the passage.

A sentence

Where would the sentence best fit?

Practice 1

Warm Up

1. What can you see in space?
2. What planets are in our solar system? Name a few.

Read the Passage

Supernovas

[■A] Supernovas are large exploding stars. [■B] They are very bright. [■C] A supernova can produce as much energy as the sun does over its whole lifetime. However, the sun is not large enough to become a supernova. [■D] A star must be nine times the weight of the sun to become a supernova.

A supernova can happen for two reasons. The first reason is that a star suddenly starts making a lot of energy. This occurs when a star gets material and gas from other stars. This gives the star more energy. Over time the energy grows until the star explodes and makes a supernova. [■E] The other reason that a supernova occurs is because a star stops producing energy. This happens when it runs out of fuel. [■F] The star becomes unable to support its size and collapses, or falls in on itself. [■G] Supernovas are so rare that they only happen about once every 50 years in a galaxy. [■H]

Target iBT TOEFL Questions

1 Look at the four squares [■A]~[■D] that indicate where the following sentence could be added to the passage.

Sometimes they shine brighter than all of the other stars in their galaxy.

Where would the sentence best fit?

2 Look at the four squares [■E]~[■H] that indicate where the following sentence could be added to the passage.

The collapsing material creates heat and light.

Where would the sentence best fit?

iBT TOEFL Vocabulary

Fill in the blanks with the appropriate words.

#	Word		Definition
1	_____	v	to burst with noise
2	_____	n	the duration of the life of someone
3	_____	adj	not able, not having the necessary skills
4	_____	v	to make, to create
5	_____	v	to break down, to fall
6	_____	adj	unusual, uncommon

- rare
- collapse
- unable
- explode
- lifetime
- produce

Astronomy •• 83

Wrap Up

A Complete the sentences with the appropriate words.

- exploded
- collapsed
- lifetime
- produced
- unable
- rare

1 When the star _____, it became the brightest star in the sky.

2 The members were _____ to change all the rules.

3 More animal species will be extinct within our _____.

4 The bridge _____ and over a hundred people died.

5 The tornadoes were _____ for this time of year.

6 The machines _____ a lot of noise.

B Complete the summary note of the passage <Supernovas>.

- A supernova is a large and b_____ exploding star.
- A supernova can happen when
    (1) a star that comes to have a lot of e_____
        → explodes and makes a supernova
    (2) a star s_____ producing energy
        → the star becomes unable to support its s_____
        → c_____ and makes a supernova
- A supernova is a r_____ phenomenon.
    → it can happen about once every _____ years.

Practice 2

Warm Up

1 Go through the passage quickly to find these words. Use what you know about these words to guess the topic.

- gravity
- space
- astronauts
- weightless

2 Identify the topic and read the passage quickly. What do you think the passage is about?

- The history of space travel ○
- What happens to the human body in space ○

Read the Passage

Your time (1st): ___ min, (2nd): ___ min

Humans in Space

The human body has adapted to Earth's gravity. Gravity is what keeps our feet on the ground every day. In space there is no gravity. Astronauts must adapt to being totally weightless. [■A] The first space flight was only 108 minutes long. [■B] On short flights, human bodies don't have many problems. [■C] Over longer periods, the effect of being weightless can be serious. [■D]

One of the effects of being weightless is losing too much water from the body. Sleeping trouble is also common during space travel. Muscles and bones also get smaller and weaker. This is because there is no gravity. In space, the blood in the body doesn't move well either. With no gravity, body fluid moves to the upper body and head. [■E] This strange balance of fluid confuses the body. Because of this, the movement of blood slows. [■F] To prevent serious problems, astronauts must eat healthy foods, drink a lot of water, and exercise. [■G] After returning to Earth, most astronauts have problems balancing, and many can't even walk. [■H]

Target iBT TOEFL Questions

1 Look at the four squares [■A]~[■D] that indicate where the following sentence could be added to the passage.

Since that time, space missions have become longer.

Where would the sentence best fit?

2 Look at the four squares [■E]~[■H] that indicate where the following sentence could be added to the passage.

Luckily, the negative effects of being weightless disappear over time.

Where would the sentence best fit?

iBT TOEFL Vocabulary

Fill in the blanks with the appropriate words.

#	Word		Definition
1	_____	n	a person who travels in space
2	_____	n	the region beyond the Earth's atmosphere
3	_____	adj	not feeling the effects of gravity
4	_____	v	to change to fit a different situation
5	_____	v	to make something unclear

- adapt
- weightless
- space
- confuse
- astronaut

Wrap Up

A Complete the sentences with the appropriate words.

- adapt
- space
- astronaut
- weightless
- confused

1. The teacher _____ the students by asking so many questions.

2. Neil Armstrong was the first _____ on the moon.

3. The human body can adjust for a _____ condition in space.

4. It is not easy to _____ to the changes.

5. There is a possibility of life in _____ .

B Complete the summary note of the passage <Humans in Space>.

Astronauts must a_____ to the w_____ condition in space.

- The effects of being weightless:
    (1) losing w_____ from the body
    (2) sleeping trouble
    (3) muscles and bones get smaller and w_____
    (4) the blood moves s_____

- To prevent serious problems
    (1) eat h_____ foods
    (2) drink a lot of water
    (3) exercise

Test 1

Jupiter

[■A] Jupiter is very far from the sun. [■B] It is the fifth planet from the sun. It takes twelve years for Jupiter to travel once around the sun. [■C] This is twelve times longer than it takes the Earth. [■D] It is 1321 times bigger than the Earth. However, only 318 Earths could fit inside Jupiter. Jupiter is made only of gas and liquid. There is no land or rock on Jupiter.

The environment of Jupiter is not very nice. If a spaceship went inside the clouds of Jupiter, it would be crushed like paper. NASA sent the "Galileo probe" to Jupiter in 1989. It took six years for the probe to get to Jupiter. In 1995, the probe went into the clouds of Jupiter. It was crushed in 59 minutes. However, it gave humans their first look at the inside environment of Jupiter.

One of Jupiter's most famous features is the Great Red Spot. This giant spot is a huge storm the size of three Earths. The storm has lasted for hundreds of years. For these reasons, Jupiter is not a very "friendly" planet.

* probe: a machine sent into space to collect information about the objects in space

---

1 Look at the four squares [■] that indicate where the following sentence could be added to the passage.

Jupiter is also the largest planet in the Milky Way.

Where would the sentence best fit?

2 The word It in the passage refers to

Ⓐ spaceship　　　Ⓑ NASA　　　Ⓒ Jupiter　　　Ⓓ probe

3 According to the passage, which of the following is NOT true of Jupiter?

Ⓐ It is bigger than the Earth.
Ⓑ It has a big red spot.
Ⓒ It has beautiful clouds.
Ⓓ It contains no land or rocks.

4 Which of the following best expresses the essential information in the highlighted sentence in the passage? Incorrect answer choices change the meaning in important ways or leave out essential information.

<mark>If a spaceship went inside the clouds of Jupiter, it would be crushed like paper.</mark>

Ⓐ Paper spaceships have gone into Jupiter's clouds.
Ⓑ Inside Jupiter's clouds, spaceships look like paper.
Ⓒ Spaceships are easily destroyed inside Jupiter's clouds.
Ⓓ Spaceships crush Jupiter's clouds like paper.

5 The author mentions <mark>three Earths</mark> in paragraph 3 in order to

Ⓐ emphasize the huge size of the red spot
Ⓑ reveal the small size of the Earth
Ⓒ show the danger of the storm
Ⓓ present the quality of the Earth

6 Why does the author say <mark>Jupiter is not a very "friendly" planet</mark>?

Ⓐ To argue that people do not like Jupiter
Ⓑ To show Jupiter's difficult environment
Ⓒ To display the size of Jupiter's storm
Ⓓ To highlight that Jupiter is a beautiful place

More to know 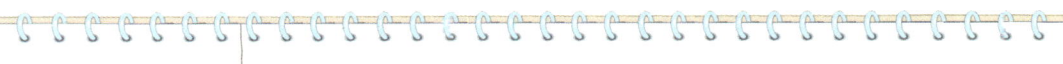 **Facts about Mars**

1. Astronomers believe that Mars once had water and a blue sky, like the Earth. However, it is unlikely that it had plants.
2. Mars has seasons like the Earth.
3. The sun appears to be about half as big from Mars as it does from the Earth.
4. The largest volcano in the solar system is on Mars.

Astronomy •• 89

Test 2

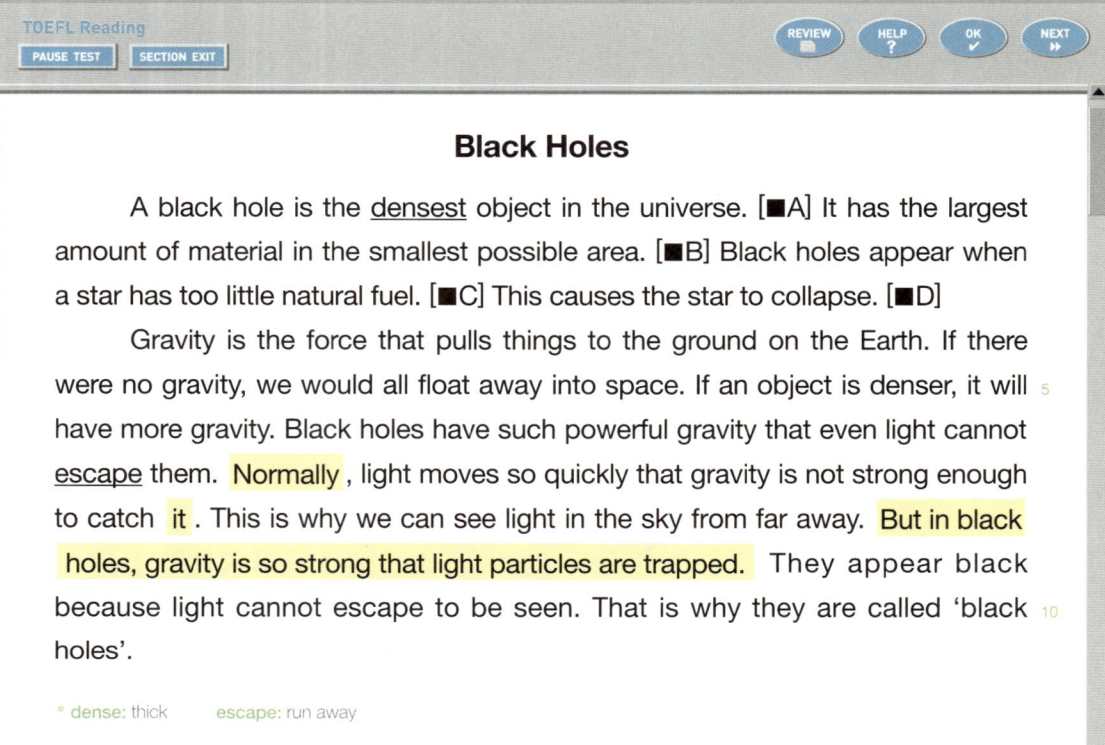

1. Look at the four squares [■] that indicate where the following sentence could be added to the passage.

   Without the fuel, the star cannot support its own weight.

   Where would the sentence best fit?

2. The word Normally in the passage is closest in meaning to
   Ⓐ totally   Ⓑ clearly   Ⓒ naturally   Ⓓ generally

3 The word it in the passage refers to

Ⓐ space Ⓑ object Ⓒ light Ⓓ gravity

4 According to the passage, which of the following is NOT true of black holes?

Ⓐ They have strong gravity.
Ⓑ They keep light.
Ⓒ They are made when a star runs out of fuel.
Ⓓ They are huge in size.

5 Which of the following best expresses the essential information in the highlighted sentence in the passage? Incorrect answer choices change the meaning in important ways or leave out essential information.

But in black holes, gravity is so strong that light particles are trapped.

Ⓐ However, light cannot escape black holes due to their strong gravity.
Ⓑ But black holes use gravity to keep light.
Ⓒ Black holes are strong because light particles cannot move around in them.
Ⓓ Although light particles cannot escape, black holes become strong.

More to know  **Amazing Facts about Black Holes**

1. Astronomers say that at least one black hole is born every day.
2. The nearest black hole to the Earth is 1,600 light years away.
3. Black holes may not be totally black.
4. There may be millions of black holes in the Galaxy.

Reading Helper

A. so [adjective/adverb] that

Examples from the passage

- Supernovas are **so** [rare] **that** they only happen about once every 50 years in a galaxy.

  (Supernovas, Line 13)

- Normally, light moves **so** [quickly] **that** gravity is not strong enough to catch it.

  (Black Holes, Line 7)

- But in black holes, gravity is **so** [strong] **that** light particles are trapped.

  (Black Holes, Line 8)

B. such [(a/an)+adjective+noun] that

Examples from the passage

- Black holes have **such** [powerful gravity] **that** even light cannot escape them.

  (Black Holes, Line 6)

Join the two sentences together to form one sentence using *so...that* or *such...that*.

1 Technology has changed fast. It's difficult to keep up.

→ Technology has changed __so__ fast __that__ it is difficult to keep up.

2 The museum was in a bad condition. It was necessary to build a new one.

→ The museum was in __such__ a bad condition __that__ it was necessary to build a new one.

3 The tornado passed quickly. It was over in an hour.

→ The tornado passed __so__ quickly __that__ it was over in an hour.

4 The book was a success. It was translated into 10 different languages.

→ The book was __such__ a big success __that__ it was translated into 10 different languages.

5 The book became popular. It was made into a movie.

→ The book became __so__ popular __that__ it was made into a movie.

UNIT 07 Arts

•• Search! Search!

Find out about the topics using the Internet.
Statues of David, Opera, Musical, Oil painting, Watercolor painting

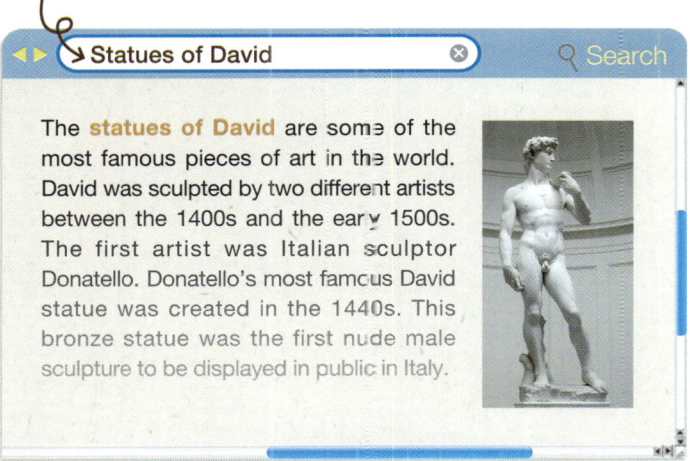

Statues of David

The **statues of David** are some of the most famous pieces of art in the world. David was sculpted by two different artists between the 1400s and the early 1500s. The first artist was Italian sculptor Donatello. Donatello's most famous David statue was created in the 1440s. This bronze statue was the first nude male sculpture to be displayed in public in Italy.

•• Target iBT TOEFL Questions

Categorization Questions

Directions: Complete the table below about the two types of _____ discussed in the passage. Match the appropriate statements to the types of _____ with which they are associated. Two of the answer choices will NOT be used.

Answer Choices

Ⓐ ~ Ⓖ

Category 1
- _____
- _____
- _____

Category 2
- _____
- _____

Practice 1

Warm Up

1 Read the passage quickly. What are the two things that are being compared?

- The statue of David and the statue of Liberty ○
- Michelangelo's David and Donatello's David ○

Read the Passage

Your time (1st): ___ min, (2nd): ___ min

Statues of David

The statues of David are some of the most famous pieces of art in the world. David was sculpted by two different artists between the 1400s and the early 1500s. The first artist was Italian sculptor Donatello. Donatello's most famous David statue was created in the 1440s. This bronze statue was the first nude male sculpture to be displayed in public in Italy. Donatello's David is wearing only boots and a hat. He is holding a large sword. He stands with his foot on the head of the giant Goliath. He had just killed Goliath. The statue shows David as a successful fighter. However, Donatello gave him a beautiful, feminine body. Some people think this was to show God's will in David's success.

Later, famous Italian painter and sculptor Michelangelo also created a statue of David. This statue was sculpted from a kind of stone called "marble." Michelangelo's David has become known as a symbol of artistic perfection around the world. It was first revealed in 1504. Michelangelo sculpted David completely nude. The form of Michelangelo's David is considered to show the beauty and strength of youth. Michelangelo's goal was to imitate <u>divine</u> creation.

* **divine:** god-like

Target iBT TOEFL Questions

1 Directions: Complete the table below about the statues of David. Match the appropriate phrases to the statue with which they are associated. TWO of the answer choices will NOT be used.

Answer Choices

Ⓐ was found in the early 1440s
Ⓑ is a symbol of artistic perfection
Ⓒ was made to represent divine creation
Ⓓ is a bronze statue
Ⓔ looks like the giant Goliath
Ⓕ displays young beauty and strength
Ⓖ represents God's wishes

Michelangelo's David

- _____
- _____
- _____

Donatello's David

- _____
- _____

iBT TOEFL Vocabulary

Fill in the blanks with the appropriate words.

#		
1	**v**	to show
2	**n**	wish or desire
3	**adj**	ending well
4	**v**	to make known, to uncover
5	**adv**	perfectly, entirely
6	**v**	to follow as an example or a model

- imitate
- completely
- reveal
- display
- will
- successful

Wrap Up

A Complete the sentences with the appropriate words.

• displayed	• imitate	• completely
• reveals	• will	• successful

1 The rumor was _____ false.

2 The research _____ details of Mars.

3 Children tend to _____ their parents' behaviors.

4 The paintings were _____ at the art gallery.

5 Everybody has the _____ to succeed in his or her life.

6 The new program has produced _____ results.

B Read the passage <Statues of David> again and write the correct name of the artist next to each picture. Then write key words that describe each statue.

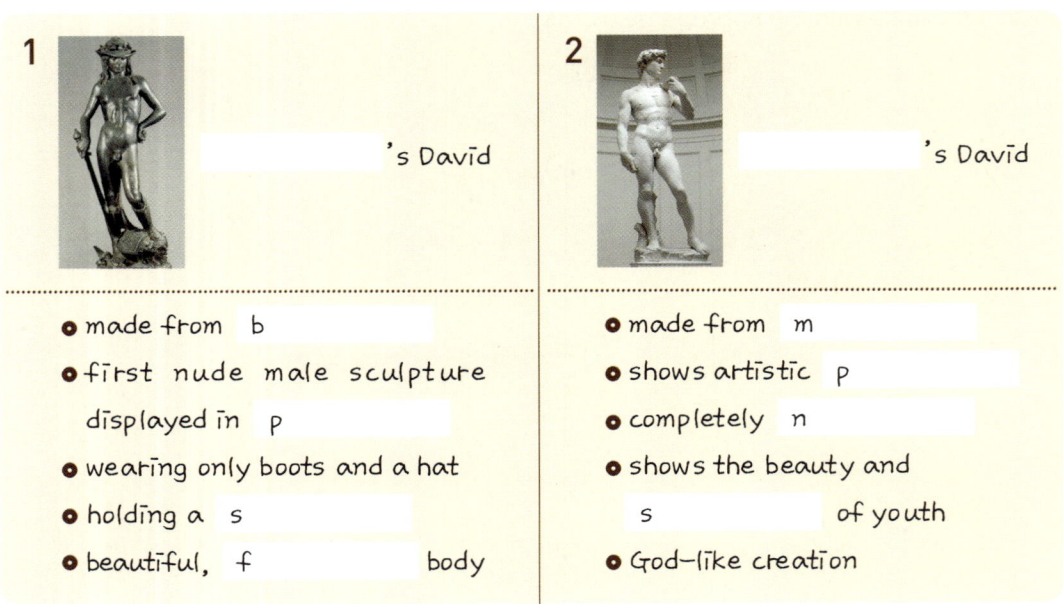

1 _____ 's David
- made from b _____
- first nude male sculpture displayed in p _____
- wearing only boots and a hat
- holding a s _____
- beautiful, f _____ body

2 _____ 's David
- made from m _____
- shows artistic p _____
- completely n _____
- shows the beauty and s _____ of youth
- God-like creation

Practice 2

Warm Up

1 Go through the passage quickly to find these words. Use what you know about these words to guess the topic.

- photography
- mass product
- advertise
- sell

2 Read the passage quickly. What are the two things that are being compared?

- Fine art photography vs. mass product photography ○
- Low-quality photos vs. high-quality photos ○

Read the Passage

Your time (1st): ____ min, (2nd): ____ min

Photography

Is photography a fine art or a mass product? Fine arts are produced mainly to show beauty. A mass product is created to sell in large amounts to make money. Some people think photography can be both a fine art and a mass product.

Photographs are often mass produced in magazines, calendars, and postcards. These photos are mainly used to advertise and sell products. They are usually carefully planned to help products sell.

Some photographers take high-quality photos and then sell them as a fine art. They are produced in small numbers. They express the view of the photographer. They also express the beauty of the subject. Often, these photos are displayed in art galleries. Their subjects are often carefully positioned for artistic effect. Fine-art photographers sometimes publish books containing their photos. These books help them make money to support new projects.

Target iBT TOEFL Questions

1 Directions: Complete the table below about the two types of photography. Match the appropriate phrases to the types of photography with which they are associated. TWO of the answer choices will NOT be used.

Answer Choices

Ⓐ is used to sell things
Ⓑ is shown in galleries
Ⓒ is produced in small numbers
Ⓓ is always published in books
Ⓔ is old-fashioned
Ⓕ is meant to show beauty and the photographer's view
Ⓖ is mostly about making money

Fine Art Photography

- _____
- _____
- _____

Mass Product Photography

- _____
- _____

iBT TOEFL Vocabulary

Fill in the blanks with the appropriate words.

1 _____	**v**	to give information to the public
2 _____	**v**	to put into a certain place
3 _____	**adj**	done in large quantities
4 _____	**adv**	for the most part
5 _____	**v**	to have the intention to do something

- mass
- plan
- mainly
- position
- advertise

Wrap Up

A Complete the sentences with the appropriate words.

- mass
- plan
- mainly
- positioned
- advertise

1 E-mails are used to _____ a product these days.

2 India is _____ to be a bridge between Asia and Europe.

3 It is important to _____ ahead when travelling.

4 The discussion was _____ about the role of parents.

5 A good example of _____ production is the car industry.

B Complete the summary note of the passage <Photography> using the words in the box.

- small
- advertise
- calendars
- beauty
- large
- photographer

Paragraph 1: Photography can be a fine art or a mass product.

Paragraph 2: Mass Product Photography
- Produced in _____ numbers
- Produced in magazines, _____, and postcards
- Used to _____ and sell products

Paragraph 3: Fine Art Photography
- High-quality photos
- Produced in _____ numbers
- Expresses the view of the _____, the _____ of the subject
- Displayed in art galleries

Arts •• 101

Test 1

Operas vs. Musicals

The histories and qualities of musicals and operas are unique. Opera began in Italy in the 16th century. It became popular throughout Europe at the time. Singing opera requires a lot of training. Opera singers don't use microphones. The singers must send their voices throughout large halls. Most operas do not include any dialogue without music. Opera is considered a distinguished art form all over Europe and the western world.

Musicals are a newer type of performance art. The first modern-style musical was performed in New York in 1866. Musical theater is a recent American invention. Unlike operas, musicals combine singing with normal dialogue and dancing. The type of music normally used in musicals is modern rock, pop, or electronic music. This music is adapted for dialogue style lyrics. Lyrics are the words used in music. The stories of musicals are often about modern day subjects. They also tend to be somewhat funny.

It's easy to find the difference between a musical and an opera. Musicals are mainly designed and enjoyed as easy entertainment while operas are a classical form of art designed to increase artistic education.

distinguished: widely known and esteemed   *combine:* add together

---

1 The word recent in the passage is closest in meaning to
   Ⓐ new   Ⓑ important   Ⓒ careful   Ⓓ exciting

2 The word They in the passage refers to
   Ⓐ lyrics   Ⓑ words   Ⓒ stories   Ⓓ subjects

3 According to the passage, which of the following is NOT true of musicals?

Ⓐ Musicals started in New York.
Ⓑ Musicals are mostly for entertainment.
Ⓒ Musicals use all kinds of music.
Ⓓ Musicals use dialogue, music, and dance.

4 What is the function of paragraph 3 as it relates to the rest of the passage?

Ⓐ It describes musical and opera singing.
Ⓑ It summarizes the main purpose of musicals and operas.
Ⓒ It highlights how musicals developed through making better performances.
Ⓓ It shows the results of music history.

5 Directions: Complete the table below about the two types of performance art. Match the appropriate phrases to the types of performance art. TWO of the answer choices will NOT be used.

Answer Choices

Ⓐ use songs, lyrics, and dance
Ⓑ do not use a microphone
Ⓒ do not require a lot of training
Ⓓ are from Europe
Ⓔ use a strange style of lyrics
Ⓕ are very respected
Ⓖ use normal dialogue

Operas
- _____
- _____
- _____

Musicals
- _____
- _____

More to know — **Broadway Musicals**

New York's Broadway is famous for its musicals. Broadway musicals sell over one and a half billion dollars' worth of tickets every year. Some of the famous Broadway musicals are;

Cats	Miss Saigon
Mamma Mia	42nd Street
Les Misérables	Chicago

Arts •• **103**

Watercolor vs. Oil Painting

Watercolor painting began with cave paintings. It started in the area that is now Europe. These paintings were done in the Paleolithic period (2,000,000 BC-10,000 BC). Ancient Egyptians also used watercolors to decorate pyramids. In early Asia, only black ink was used for a special type of writing. It was called "calligraphy". Traditional Asian paintings used similar watercolors to make dark outlines of natural scenes. Watercolor painting became famous again in the 15th century. The German painter Albrecht Durer started using it then. Watercolor paints usually produce soft tones. They also limit the definition of edges in pictures.

Oil painting dates back to the Roman Empire, from 753 BC to 509 BC. Research shows that oil painting appeared in Asia between the 5th and the 9th centuries. It is believed that oil painting first became popular in the Netherlands in the 15th century. From there, oil painting spread through the rest of Northern Europe and then to Italy. [■A] Oil painting became a popular method for a number of important reasons. [■B] First, oil paints provide richer colors and a sharper contrast of colors. [■C] Second, oil paints take a long time to dry, which allows painters to correct errors more easily. [■D]

* **Paleolithic:** early stage of the Stone Age

---

1 The word famous in the passage is closest in meaning to

Ⓐ different　　Ⓑ popular　　Ⓒ colorful　　Ⓓ clear

2 According to paragraph 1, calligraphy

Ⓐ uses only one color
Ⓑ was first introduced by a German painter
Ⓒ is used to make pictures of nature
Ⓓ began in the Paleolithic period

3 The word errors in the passage is closest in meaning to

　Ⓐ lines　　　　　Ⓑ habits　　　　　Ⓒ examples　　　　　Ⓓ mistakes

4 According to the passage, oil painting

　Ⓐ began earlier than watercolor painting
　Ⓑ was most popular in the 15th century
　Ⓒ began in the Netherlands
　Ⓓ takes a long time to dry

5 Look at the four squares [■] that indicate where the following sentence could be added to the passage.

Some art experts believe that oil paints are not completely dry until 60-80 years have passed.

Where would the sentence best fit?

6 Directions: Complete the table below about the two types of painting. Match the appropriate phrases to the types of painting with which they are associated. TWO of the answer choices will NOT be used.

Answer Choices

　Ⓐ was used by ancient humans
　Ⓑ was popular in Northern Europe
　Ⓒ was invented by Egyptians
　Ⓓ uses soft tones and edges
　Ⓔ was created in the Netherlands
　Ⓕ gives rich colors and contrast
　Ⓖ is used for calligraphy

Watercolor Painting

- _____
- _____
- _____

Oil Painting

- _____
- _____

Reading Helper

A. help... do...

Examples from the passage
- They are usually carefully planned to **help** products **sell**. (Photography, Line 6)
- These books **help** them **make** money to support new projects. (Photography, Line 13)

Rearrange the words to complete the sentences.

1. People can (the / help / drought / survive / the / animals)
   → People can _____ .

2. The new program (time / help / teachers / save / will / the)
   → The new program _____ .

3. Taking care of a pet can (help / social skills / children / develop)
   → Taking care of a pet can _____ .

4. Good friends may (your / longer / life / last / help)
   → Good friends may _____ .

B. it is easy / difficult / important to…

> **Examples from the passage**
> • **It's easy to** find the difference between a musical and an opera.
>
> (Operas vs. Musicals, Line 14)

Correct the mistakes in the sentences.

1 It is important find main ideas when you are reading.

2 It is difficult learning a foreign language.

Complete the sentences using the words given.

3 (difficult, a, is, leader, it, to, be) if you are inexperienced in dealing with people.

→

4 (important, goals, is, specific, it, to, have) in life.

→

5 (is, club, the, to, join, easy, it, very)

→

UNIT 08
Architecture

• Search! Search!

Find out about the topics using the Internet.
Notre Dame de Paris, Tall Towers, North American Indian Houses, Renaissance Architecture

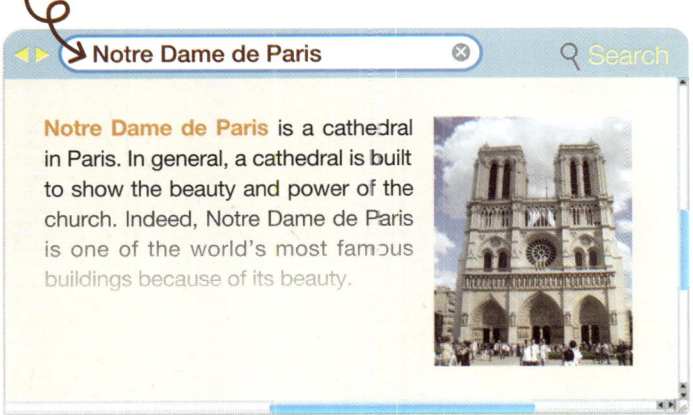

• Target iBT TOEFL Questions

Summary Questions

Directions: An introductory sentence for a brief summary of the passage is provided below. Complete the summary by selecting the THREE answer choices that express important ideas in the passage. Some sentences do not belong in the summary because they express ideas that are not presented in the passage or are minor ideas in the passage.

An introductory sentence

-
-
-

Answer Choices

Ⓐ ~ Ⓕ

Practice 1

Warm Up

1. Can you identify which is the Eiffel Tower and which is Notre Dame Cathedral?

2. What do you know about each building?

Read the Passage

Your time (1st): ___ min, (2nd): ___ min

Notre Dame de Paris

Notre Dame de Paris is a cathedral in Paris. In general, a cathedral is built to show the beauty and power of the church. Indeed, Notre Dame de Paris is one of the world's most famous buildings because of its beauty.

Notre Dame Cathedral is a good example of a gothic building. Gothic-style buildings have several common features. First, they focus on lines going up and down. For this reason, gothic buildings have tall, pointed towers and arches. Arches are shaped like half-eggs. They are often used for the tops of doorways. Gothic arches, however, have sharp pointed tops. Second, gothic style focuses on light. For lots of light, it uses many large windows often decorated with stained glass.

The west side of Notre Dame Cathedral is famous for its two towers. These towers are 69 meters tall. Between the towers, there is a circular stained-glass window. This 10-meter window is called "The West Rose." A statue of the Virgin Mary stands with Baby Jesus in front of the window.

Construction of Notre Dame de Paris began in 1163. It took until 1345 to complete. Despite being over 800 years old, Notre Dame Cathedral is still a powerful Roman Catholic church.

Target iBT TOEFL Questions

1 Directions: An introductory sentence for a brief summary of the passage is provided below. Complete the summary by selecting the THREE answer choices that best express important ideas in the passage. Some sentences do not belong in the summary because they express ideas that are not presented in the passage or are minor ideas in the passage.

Notre Dame Cathedral is a famous building in Paris.

-
-
-

Answer Choices

Ⓐ It is famous for its gothic architecture.
Ⓑ It has sharp pointed tops.
Ⓒ It is well-known for its two towers and a circular stained-glass window.
Ⓓ It took almost 200 years to build.
Ⓔ The construction began in 1345.

iBT TOEFL Vocabulary

Fill in the blanks with the appropriate words.

1	**adj** more than two or three
2	**n** a special characteristic
3	**v** to make something beautiful by adding color or ornament
4	**v** to give a certain form to
5	**v** to finish
6	**prep** in spite of, regardless of

- feature
- despite
- several
- shape
- decorate
- complete

Wrap Up

A Complete the sentences with the appropriate words.

> - feature
> - decorated
> - shaped
> - complete
> - despite
> - several

1 The use of dark colors is the well-known _____ of his paintings.

2 _____ heavy rain, many people gathered for the parade.

3 It took twenty years to _____ the building.

4 Some of the stones are _____ like animals.

5 The children _____ the Christmas tree.

6 There are _____ ways to solve this problem.

B Complete the summary of the passage <Notre Dame de Paris>.

> Notre Dame de Paris is a famous cathedral in P_____. It is a good e_____ of a gothic building. Gothic buildings have tall, pointed towers and arches. And they have stained-glass windows. C_____ of Notre Dame de Paris began in 1163 and was completed in _____. It has two towers and there is a circular stained-glass window between them. Although it is more than _____ years old, Notre Dame Cathedral is still a powerful Roman C_____ church.

Practice 2

Warm Up

1 Go through the passage quickly to find the names of the two buildings mentioned.

2 Identify the topic and read the passage quickly. What do you think the passage is about?

- Steel and poles ○
- Tall buildings ○

Read the Passage

Your time (1st): ____ min, (2nd): ____ min

Tall Towers

In the early 1900s, buildings started getting much taller. This change was due to new building materials. Steel was introduced at that time. It was the strongest of materials. The strength of steel made it possible to build tall buildings. Tall buildings use huge steel poles. They stand like legs through a building. Each steel pole has a huge base. The bases prevent the steel poles from sinking into the ground. This is very impressive because these buildings are very heavy.

For tall buildings, the wind can be a very dangerous force. Strong winds can blow a building over. So, engineers found ways to beat the wind. In older buildings, the steel near the outside of the building was made weaker to be more flexible. The Empire State Building was built this way. Buildings with a strong steel <u>core</u> can move with the wind.

In newer buildings, a computer system handles the wind. Buildings such as the Petronas Towers in Malaysia use computers to monitor the wind. On top of the buildings are big concrete weights that move on tracks. When the computer senses a wind change, the weight is moved to help balance the building.

* **core:** the center of an object

Target iBT TOEFL Questions

1 Directions: An introductory sentence for a brief summary of the passage is provided below. Complete the summary by selecting the THREE answer choices that best express important ideas in the passage. Some sentences do not belong in the summary because they express ideas that are not presented in the passage or are minor ideas in the passage.

Buildings began getting taller thanks to new building materials and technology.

-
-
-

Answer Choices

Ⓐ Tall buildings use huge steel legs and huge bases.
Ⓑ New tall buildings use computers to monitor wind changes and move buildings according to the wind.
Ⓒ Engineers use wind to balance buildings.
Ⓓ Older buildings use steel poles' strength to handle wind.
Ⓔ Buildings started getting taller and taller.

iBT TOEFL Vocabulary

Fill in the blanks with the appropriate words.

#	Word		Definition
1		**v**	to stop, to block, to prohibit
2		**adj**	able to adjust to different conditions
3		**v**	to manage, to control
4		**v**	to watch and check
5		**v**	to be equal, to make equal

- handle
- flexible
- monitor
- prevent
- balance

Wrap Up

A Fill in the blanks with the appropriate words.

- handle
- monitored
- balance
- flexible
- prevented

1 The situation should be _____ carefully.

2 The new plan _____ the economy from growing.

3 The plans are _____ : They can be changed when necessary.

4 There is no need to _____ the power between the two groups.

5 Students need to know how to _____ their problems.

B Where would the sentences fit best in the summary of the passage <Tall Towers>? Write the appropriate letter next to each sentence.

1 Tall buildings use huge steel poles and huge bases. ____

2 When a wind change is sensed, the weight is moved to balance the building. ____

   In the early 1900s, buildings started getting much taller due to a new building material called steel. (A) The huge bases prevent the steel poles from sinking into the ground. (B) For tall buildings, the wind can be very dangerous. (C) So, in older buildings such as the Empire State Building, the steel near the outside of the building was made weaker to be more flexible. (D) In newer buildings, such as the Petronas Towers in Malaysia, a computer system is used to monitor the wind. (E)

North American Indian Houses

American Indians built their homes using the natural materials around them. North America has many different climates. Due to the many climates in North America, Native Indians built different types of houses. The type of house depended on the type of climate.

In Northwestern America, the winter climate is cold. Indians in this area built wooden homes, and families lived together in the homes. In winter, living together kept each family warm. These wooden homes were called "longhouses." Longhouses were large, rectangle-shaped buildings. The wood frame was built first. Then it was covered with long, flat pieces of wood. The families in a longhouse would share the fire in the center of the house for cooking.

On the other hand, the Southwest area of America is usually very hot and dry. The Indians of this area built large apartment-like buildings. These buildings would hold many apartments where each family lived separately. Apartments were added as the number of families increased. Southwestern Indian buildings were made of adobe. Adobe is a type of brick, and it is made from sun-dried clay and plant material.

* **climate:** the average weather of an area

Northwest Indian House

Southwest Indian House

1 The word center in the passage is closest in meaning to

Ⓐ end Ⓑ middle Ⓒ focus Ⓓ place

2 According to paragraph 2, which of the following is NOT true of longhouses?

Ⓐ They were a special type of housing for winter.
Ⓑ They had a rectangular shape.
Ⓒ They were made of wood.
Ⓓ They had a fireplace in the center.

3 According to paragraphs 1 and 2, it can be inferred that

Ⓐ the winter climate in Northwestern America is mild
Ⓑ the Northwestern area is likely to have many trees
Ⓒ Northwestern Indians enjoy living together
Ⓓ all American Indians live in large, wooden houses

4 Directions: An introductory sentence for a brief summary of the passage is provided below. Complete the summary by selecting the THREE answer choices that best express important ideas in the passage. Some sentences do not belong in the summary because they express ideas that are not presented in the passage or are minor ideas in the passage.

North American Indian homes changed according to the climate and environment.
-
-
-

Answer Choices

Ⓐ Indians in cold climates lived together in large houses.
Ⓑ Indians in cold climates had many families.
Ⓒ To build their houses, Northwest Indians used wood while Southwest Indians used adobe.
Ⓓ Northwest Indians lived together so they could eat together.
Ⓔ Southwest Indians made houses of clay and ate plants
Ⓕ In the Southwest, each family lived seperately in the apartment-like buildings due to their hot climate.

Test 2

Renaissance Architecture

The word *renaissance* is French for "rebirth" or "to be born again." The Renaissance Period was a time when ancient Greek and Roman architecture was widespread for a second time. This period was from the early 15th century to the early 17th century. In this time, architects focused on Greek and Roman principles of building. These principles included symmetry. This means that the parts of a building's design are balanced.

Renaissance architects also made some changes, like using brick for building. Art was also a new addition to the Renaissance version of ancient architecture. Renaissance builders worked with artists to include wall paintings and sculptures in the design of their buildings. As a result, famous artists like Michelangelo and Leonardo Da Vinci contributed to Renaissance architecture.

[■A] The birthplace of Renaissance architecture was Florence, Italy. From Florence, it spread to other parts of Italy, such as Rome and Milan. [■B] It reached France 125 years after it began in Florence. [■C] Although the styles changed slightly throughout Europe, the basic ideas remained the same. [■D] A common sight on many Renaissance buildings is a dome, or half-circle shaped roof.

* principle: rule, standard

1 The word **widespread** in the passage is closest in meaning to
  Ⓐ popular   Ⓑ outstanding   Ⓒ possible   Ⓓ weak

2 The word **their** in the passage refers to
  Ⓐ builders   Ⓑ artists   Ⓒ wall paintings   Ⓓ sculptures

3 Which of the following best expresses the essential information in the highlighted sentence in the passage? Incorrect answer choices change the meaning in important ways or leave out essential information.

> Although the styles changed slightly throughout Europe, the basic ideas remained the same.

Ⓐ European style changed the principles of Renaissance architecture.

Ⓑ Although a little different in each place, Renaissance architecture was similar throughout Europe.

Ⓒ Renaissance architecture changed the style of Europe.

Ⓓ In Europe, the basic rules and styles became a little different in each place.

4 Look at the four squares [■] that indicate where the following sentence could be added to the passage.

Then it spread to other parts of Europe.

Where would the sentence best fit?

5 **Directions**: An introductory sentence for a brief summary of the passage is provided below. Complete the summary by selecting the THREE answer choices that best express important ideas in the passage. Some sentences do not belong in the summary because they express ideas that are not presented in the passage or are minor ideas in the passage.

The Renaissance was an influential style movement that swept through Europe.

-
-
-

Answer Choices

Ⓐ The architects were Greek and Roman.

Ⓑ The architecture used Greek and Roman principles.

Ⓒ Renaissance buildings included paintings and other art.

Ⓓ Renaissance buildings were made by Michelangelo.

Ⓔ All Renaissance buildings have domes.

Ⓕ Renaissance architecture moved through Europe from Italy.

Reading Helper

A. due to (because of)

> **Examples from the passage**
> - This change was **due to** new building materials. (Tall Towers, Line 2)
> - **Due to** the many climates in North America, Native Indians built different types of houses. (North American Indian Houses, Line 2)

Rearrange the words to make a complete sentence.

1 The success (work / hard / to / due / was)

→ The success _____.

2 The drought (climate / change / due / was / to / the)

→ The drought _____.

3 It became easy to find resources (due/ the / largely / Internet / to)

→ It became easy to find resources _____.

4 (the / to / people / due / active / the / participation / of), the conference ended successfully

→ _____, the conference ended successfully.

B. prevent ... from -ing

Examples from the passage
- The bases **prevent** the steel poles **from sinking** into the ground. (Tall Towers, Line 6)

Complete the sentences using the expressions given.

1 The drug will prevent the disease from _____.
(develop)

2 The war prevented the people from _____.
(return to their home country)

3 Stretching will prevent you from _____.
(hurt your body)

4 The new plan prevented the school from _____.
(close)

Actual Test

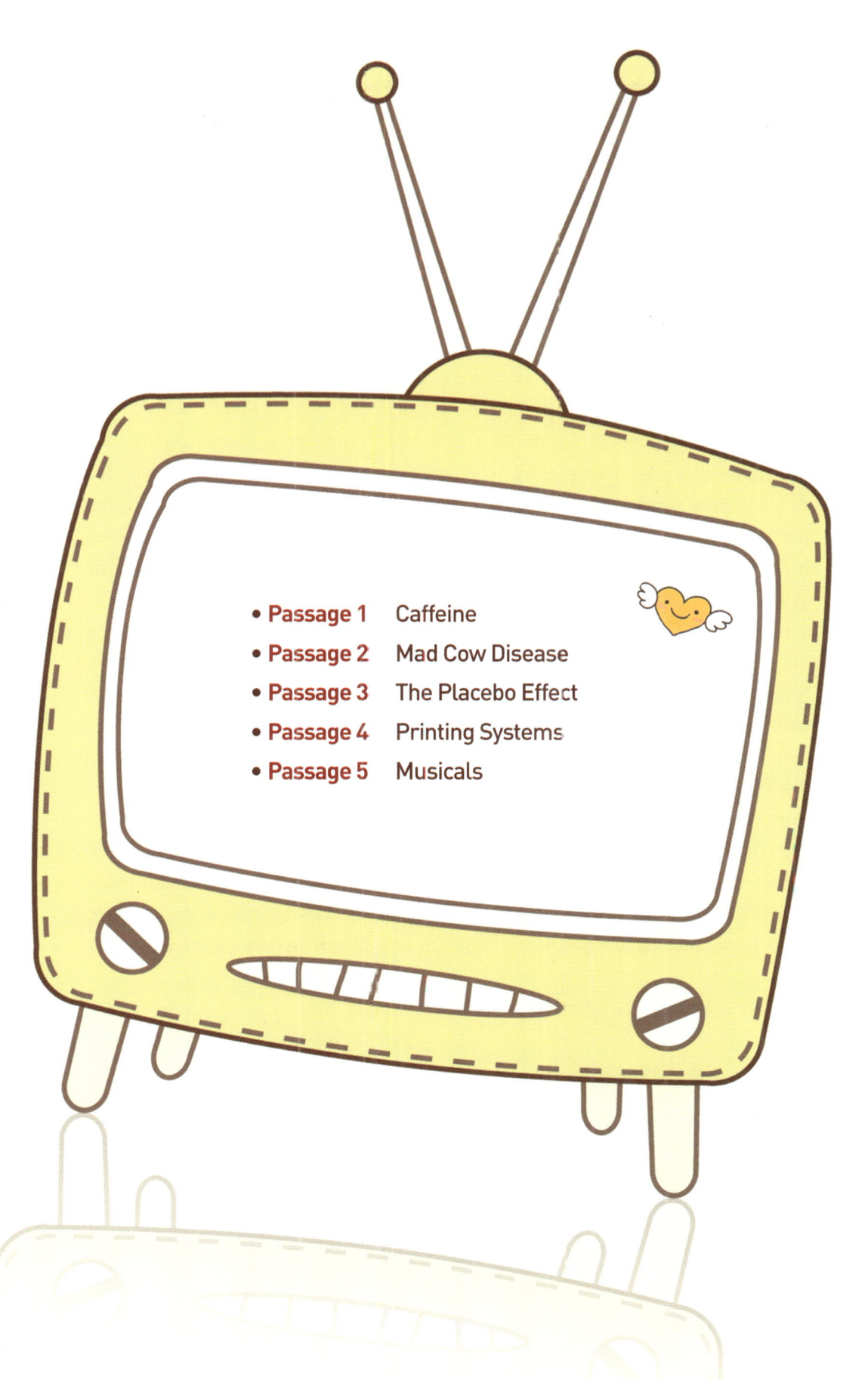

- **Passage 1** Caffeine
- **Passage 2** Mad Cow Disease
- **Passage 3** The Placebo Effect
- **Passage 4** Printing Systems
- **Passage 5** Musicals

Passage 1

Caffeine

Caffeine is the chemical in coffee. It is also in tea, chocolate and cola. Caffeine makes us feel more awake. Caffeine is the reason that coffee is a popular drink in the morning.

Caffeine increases the amount of sugar in the body. More sugar in the blood gives people more energy. This happens even if a cup of coffee or tea does not have sugar in it. Caffeine can help people to stay awake when they are tired. It can also make us move more quickly when things occur. Some studies show that it can help the heart and brain fight disease. People may even be able to run longer if they use caffeine beforehand.

Unfortunately, caffeine can also have negative effects. Too much caffeine can make people feel nervous and sick. It may also make sleeping difficult. Over long periods, a lot of caffeine can raise a person's heart rate. It can also make a person feel stressed. This can lead to heart problems later in life.

One study looked at children who drank a bottle of cola during the day. After drinking cola, the children could not sleep well. This happened even many hours later. The children also woke up more often in the night, and the next day they were tired at school. Over a long period, this could result in serious health problems for children. [■A] Sleep is important for maintaining a healthy body. [■B] Tired minds do not learn well. [■C] In small amounts caffeine can be very useful to people. [■D] However, in large amounts it can be very dangerous.

1 The word awake in the passage is closest in meaning to

Ⓐ excited
Ⓑ careful
Ⓒ open
Ⓓ attractive

2 According to paragraphs 1 and 2, which of the following is true of caffeine?

  Ⓐ It can make people run.
  Ⓑ It can help people lose weight.
  Ⓒ It makes people feel energetic.
  Ⓓ It works better with sugar.

3 Which of the following best expresses the essential information in the highlighted sentence in the passage? Incorrect choices change the meaning in important ways or leave out essential information.

  People may even be able to run longer if they use caffeine beforehand.

  Ⓐ Running is easier if you drink caffeine later.
  Ⓑ Drinking caffeine before running can help people run longer.
  Ⓒ Caffeine can help runners keep running.
  Ⓓ People drink coffee before they run in order to run longer.

4 According to paragraph 3, which of the following is NOT mentioned as negative effects of caffeine?

  Ⓐ It can make people feel nervous.
  Ⓑ It can cause headaches.
  Ⓒ It can make sleep difficult.
  Ⓓ It can cause heart problems.

5 The author mentions cola in paragraph 4 in order to

  Ⓐ show that coffee and cola are the same
  Ⓑ give an example of drinks the children like
  Ⓒ give an example of negative effects of caffeine on children
  Ⓓ show that caffeine helps kids stay awake in class

6 Look at the four squares [■] that indicate where the following sentence could be added to the passage.

  Sleep is also important for good learning.

  Where would the sentence best fit?

7 Directions: An introductory sentence for a brief summary of the passage is provided below. Complete the summary by selecting the THREE answer choices that express important ideas in the passage. Some sentences do not belong in the summary because they express ideas that are not presented in the passage or are minor ideas in the passage.

Caffeine is everywhere in today's society.

-
-
-

Answer Choices

Ⓐ Caffeine has many good effects on people.
Ⓑ Coffee with sugar gives us even more energy.
Ⓒ Too much caffeine can cause health problems.
Ⓓ Many runners use caffeine.
Ⓔ An experiment shows that children experience sleeping problems after drinking cola.
Ⓕ Sleep is important for children to be healthy.

Mad Cow Disease

Mad Cow Disease is a dangerous illness. It affects a cow's brain, causing the animal to go "mad". The word "mad" also means "strange". Cows with this disease may have trouble walking normally. Their eyes may turn red. They may also do other unusual things. They may seem very nervous and they may not be able to stand up. This happens because the disease destroys the cow's brain. Over time, the cow's brain will have holes in it like a sponge.

It is believed that Mad Cow Disease is spread when certain parts of a sick cow are eaten. The parts of a cow which can carry Mad Cow Disease are the brain and the backbone. Cows only eat grass and grain. However, the dangerous body parts were used in cattle feed and may have caused serious damage to the brains of the animals that ate it. Feed that uses these body parts was banned in 1997.

The area that had the most problems with this disease was the United Kingdom. In the United Kingdom, 179,000 cows caught Mad Cow Disease. Mad Cow Disease can also affect humans. A hundred and sixty-three people died in the United Kingdom of Mad Cow Disease. People with the disease may have memory problems. After some time, people with Mad Cow Disease will have trouble moving properly. Their bodies may shake all of a sudden. A person with this disease can last only a few weeks or months before dying.

Many researchers say the chance of getting sick from the disease is very low. We can not get it by simply being near someone with the disease. However, we still need to be careful. Cattle feed should never include the parts of cows with this disease. Above all, we should avoid eating the dangerous parts of a sick cow.

1 The word unusual in the passage is closest in meaning to

- Ⓐ special
- Ⓑ unimportant
- Ⓒ universal
- Ⓓ strange

2 According to paragraph 1, all of the following are mentioned as symptoms of Mad Cow Disease EXCEPT

- Ⓐ red eyes
- Ⓑ nervous behavior
- Ⓒ trouble standing
- Ⓓ madness

3 The word banned in the passage is closest in meaning to

- Ⓐ lowered
- Ⓑ prohibited
- Ⓒ produced
- Ⓓ sold

4 According to paragraph 2, Mad Cow Disease is spread by

- Ⓐ eating cattle feed
- Ⓑ eating the brain and the backbone of sick cows
- Ⓒ eating any beef
- Ⓓ being near sick cows

5 The word properly in the passage is closest in meaning to

- Ⓐ closely
- Ⓑ possibly
- Ⓒ quickly
- Ⓓ normally

6 The word it in the passage refers to

Ⓐ trouble
Ⓑ chance
Ⓒ disease
Ⓓ food

7 According to paragraphs 3 and 4, which of the following can be inferred about Mad Cow Disease?

Ⓐ People should not eat meat if they want to be safe from the disease.
Ⓑ It can spread people to people
Ⓒ It only occurred in the United Kingdom.
Ⓓ Cattle feed that included the parts of sick cows was used in the U.K.

8 Directions: An introductory sentence for a brief summary of the passage is provided below. Complete the summary by selecting the THREE answer choices that express important ideas in the passage. Some sentences do not belong in the summary because they express ideas that are not presented in the passage or are minor ideas in the passage.

Mad Cow Disease is an illness related to beef.

-
-
-

Answer Choices

Ⓐ It makes people crazy.
Ⓑ It causes people and cows to behave strangely.
Ⓒ It is spread by eating specific parts of sick cows.
Ⓓ It is spread by eating bad feed.
Ⓔ Not eating meat from the United Kingdom will keep people healthy.
Ⓕ Being cautious about what we eat will keep people healthy.

Passage 3

The Placebo Effect

A "placebo" is a fake treatment for sickness. In other words, placebos are not real medicines. Most placebos are made only from sugar. What's interesting is that they can actually help patients. Patients taking placebos often start to get better. Patients using placebos do not know that it is not real medicine. Doctors are able to measure the improvement of these patients.

The reason that placebos work is not completely known. There are many possible reasons for the success of placebos. Many people think placebos are helpful because patients believe in them. This means that believing in the treatment causes the patient's body to change. These changes may help fight the sickness. Some other people think the placebo effect is part of the normal healing process. They say that patients improve because they heal naturally. They say there is no help from the placebos. Another reason is that attention given to patients during treatment makes them happier and stronger. For this reason, the patient's body can fight the sickness more effectively.

There have been many studies about placebos. Some studies show a 75 percent success rate for placebos. Other studies show that placebos are the same as no treatment at all. Some doctors believe that placebos can be harmful to patients. They suggest that patients can begin to depend on them. This may be because patients think they will get sick without a placebo.

In some cases, patients get sicker with placebos. This may be because they do not believe in the treatment. This can happen with both real medicine and placebos. It is called the "nocebo effect". Patients with the nocebo effect get sicker because they don't think the treatment will work. This can happen even if they would get well naturally. It is believed that their doubt about the treatment causes this effect.

patient: a sick person getting help from a doctor

1 According to paragraph 1, which of the following is true of placebos?

Ⓐ Placebos are medicine.
Ⓑ Placebos look like sugar.
Ⓒ Placebos can help people.
Ⓓ Placebos always cure sickness.

2 The word completely in the passage is closest in meaning to

Ⓐ widely
Ⓑ fully
Ⓒ only
Ⓓ partly

3 The word them in the passage refers to

Ⓐ reasons
Ⓑ people
Ⓒ placebos
Ⓓ patients

4 According to paragraph 2, all of the following are mentioned as reasons for the success of placebos EXCEPT

Ⓐ believing in the treatment
Ⓑ natural healing
Ⓒ being happier from good attention
Ⓓ fighting the disease

5 Which of the following best expresses the essential information in the highlighted sentence in the passage? Incorrect choices change the meaning in important ways or leave out essential information.

This means that believing in the treatment causes the patient's body to change.

Ⓐ Changes in the patient's body help them to believe in the treatment.
Ⓑ Treatment helps patients believe in their body changes.
Ⓒ Believing in the treatment will change the body's function.
Ⓓ Believing in the treatment changes the body's shape.

6 The word <mark>harmful</mark> in the passage is closest in meaning to

Ⓐ dangerous
Ⓑ different
Ⓒ clear
Ⓓ unique

7 According to paragraph 3, which of the following can be inferred about research that studies placebos?

Ⓐ Research about placebo drugs has mixed results.
Ⓑ Researchers will soon find the reasons for the success of placebos.
Ⓒ Research shows placebos can kill people.
Ⓓ Researchers know placebos don't work.

8 Directions: Complete the table below about the two types of behavior discussed in the passage. Match the appropriate statements to the types of behavior with which they are associated. Two of the answer choices will NOT be used.

Answer Choices

Ⓐ helps patients get well
Ⓑ is caused by bad doctors
Ⓒ is caused by not believing
Ⓓ makes patients sicker
Ⓔ is used for healthy people
Ⓕ is not fully understood
Ⓖ is caused by believing

Placebo

- _____
- _____
- _____

Nocebo

- _____
- _____

Printing Systems

The history of printing began a long time ago. Ancient Egyptians used early woodblock printing. Around 8 AD, the Chinese printed the first book using woodblocks. Whole pages were carved into each woodblock. This method took a lot of time and effort. In the thirteenth century, the Chinese started making single character blocks. These single blocks can be used for different books. This new system made printing faster but there were still problems. Carving each wood piece took a long time. The characters were sometimes hard to read. Furthermore, the wood pieces quickly broke, so they needed to be changed often.

In Korea, metal type began to be made in the early thirteenth century. "Metal type" is the name for printing pieces made of metal. [■A] Woodblocks were pressed into sand. [■B] This left the shape of the wood character in the sand. [■C] Then liquid metal was poured into the sand. [■D] Metals such as copper, iron, and bronze were used to make this metal type. This slow system made printing special. Only rich and educated people could use printed material.

In the fifteenth century, a German named Johannes Gutenberg made important changes to metal printing. He used metal type to create a faster printing system. Gutenberg used copper instead of sand to make the type. This made the metal characters clearer. He also made a new ink for printing. The ink was made of oil, which was perfect for printing machines. Gutenberg's printing machines also made printing easier to read.

The most famous book made by Gutenberg was a bible. The Gutenberg Bible was printed 180 times. The Gutenberg Bible is a symbol of the beginning of mass-printed books. After this time, important information could be shared with many people. As Gutenberg's machine made it easy to make many copies, books and papers became available to the average people. This invention changed world history.

carve: to cut into a surface   **mass:** done in large quantities

1 The word they in the passage refers to

   Ⓐ books
   Ⓑ problems
   Ⓒ characters
   Ⓓ wood pieces

2 According to paragraph 1, which of the following is NOT mentioned about woodblock characters?

   Ⓐ They were weak.
   Ⓑ They needed to be changed often.
   Ⓒ They were sometimes difficult to read.
   Ⓓ They were easy to get wet.

3 According to paragraphs 2 and 3, it can be inferred that

   Ⓐ woodblocks had a better quality product than metal types
   Ⓑ poor people couldn't get enough information
   Ⓒ Asia and Europe used similar printing systems
   Ⓓ speed wasn't an important aspect in developing printing systems

4 According to paragraphs 3 and 4, which of the following is true of Gutenberg?

   Ⓐ He used copper and sand to make printing pieces.
   Ⓑ He made a new ink for printing.
   Ⓒ He made a new kind of woodblock.
   Ⓓ He encouraged people to read the bible.

5 Look at the four squares [■] that indicate where the following sentence could be added to the passage.

   Once the metal dried, the metal printing pieces were ready.

   Where would the sentence best fit?

6 The word average in the passage is closest in meaning to

Ⓐ common
Ⓑ educated
Ⓒ normal
Ⓓ modest

7 Which of the following best expresses the essential information in the highlighted sentence in the passage? Incorrect choices change the meaning in important ways or leave out essential information.

After this time, important information could be shared with many people.

Ⓐ After Gutenberg died, people shared his information.
Ⓑ After his printing of a bible, people understood important information and shared it.
Ⓒ After mass printing, more people could have access to important information.
Ⓓ After books, information was shared by people.

8 **Directions**: An introductory sentence for a brief summary of the passage is provided below. Complete the summary by selecting the THREE answer choices that express important ideas in the passage. Some sentences do not belong in the summary because they express ideas that are not presented in the passage or are minor ideas in the passage.

Printing has a long history.

-
-
-

Answer Choices

Ⓐ The Chinese invented printing.
Ⓑ Both the Egyptians and the Chinese used early woodblock printing.
Ⓒ A German man was the first to invent metal type for printing.
Ⓓ The Bible made printing and reading popular.
Ⓔ Metal type started to be used in Korea in the 13th century.
Ⓕ Gutenberg invented a machine that could print many books in the 15th century.

Passage 5

Musicals

Musicals are stories that include singing by actors. Musicals can be performed on stage or in movies. They may have started around the fifth century BC. The Ancient Greeks used music and dance to tell stories. These stories were performed by theater actors. Later, the Romans also began using music and dance in theater. In the Middle Ages, musicians travelled around their countries. They would stop in towns and perform musical plays. Many of these were comedies. These performances later became opera and theater musicals.

After the 1900s, musicals began to change in America. Americans started to change musical theater from its European traditions. Opera was the main European type of musical theater then. Americans began to make more happy and funny musical stories. American musical theater became very famous around the world.

In the 1930s, the cabaret became popular. A cabaret is a restaurant with live performances such as singing, dancing or comedy. Soon after, film that had sound was invented. Musicals quickly became popular movies. Roger and Hammerstein made some of the most famous early musical movies. These included *The King and I* and *The Sound of Music*. They used songs to show feelings and ideas important to the story.

In the 1960s to 1970s, many of these musicals used rock music. They were called "rock operas". [■A] Rock music is strong music. [■B] This helped show anger about problems in modern society. In the 1980s, musicals were not very common. [■C] During the early 1990s, musicals were usually about dance and art schools. [■D] Music and dancing were only used to entertain. This was different from early musicals. Early musicals used music to help tell a story. Later in the 1990s, music was used in animated movies. Disney made animated musicals such as *Beauty and the Beast* and *The Lion King*. Like earlier musicals, these movies used music to tell the story. These musical movies were very popular. Musicals that used music for storytelling became popular for a second time.

1 The word these in the passage refers to

　Ⓐ musicians
　Ⓑ towns
　Ⓒ musical plays
　Ⓓ comedies

2 The word invented in the passage is closest in meaning to

　Ⓐ created
　Ⓑ imagined
　Ⓒ built
　Ⓓ saved

3 According to paragraph 3, musical movies began when

　Ⓐ cabaret became popular
　Ⓑ sound film was invented
　Ⓒ *The Sound of Music* was written
　Ⓓ songs began to show feelings and ideas

4 Which of the following best expresses the essential information in the highlighted sentence in the passage? Incorrect choices change the meaning in important ways or leave out essential information.

They used songs to show feelings and ideas important to the story.

　Ⓐ *The King and I* showed many important ideas and feelings about music.
　Ⓑ Feelings and ideas were expressed through music in early musical movies.
　Ⓒ Songs were used in important stories about feelings and ideas.
　Ⓓ *The Sound of Music* used music to express important ideas about feelings.

5 Look at the four squares [■] that indicate where the following sentence could be added to the passage.

However, the 1990s began a new season for musicals.

Where would the sentence best fit?

6 According to paragraph 4, musicals in the 1990s were different from the musicals of the past in that

  Ⓐ they were popular
  Ⓑ they were mostly comedies
  Ⓒ they were made into movies
  Ⓓ they used music only for entertaining

7 According to the passage, which of the following is NOT true of musicals?

  Ⓐ Musicals can be performed on stage or in movies.
  Ⓑ Modern musicals were adapted from opera.
  Ⓒ Musicals were popular throughout the 1900s.
  Ⓓ Recent musicals use the same type of storytelling as early musicals did.

8 Directions: An introductory sentence for a brief summary of the passage is provided below. Complete the summary by selecting the THREE answer choices that express important ideas in the passage. Some sentences do not belong in the summary because they express ideas that are not presented in the passage or are minor ideas in the passage.

In America, musicals have changed throughout the 1900s.

-
-
-

Answer Choices

  Ⓐ Musicals were invented in Greece.
  Ⓑ Musicals became movies in the 1930s with the beginning of sound films.
  Ⓒ In the 1960s and 1970s, many musicals began to use rock music.
  Ⓓ Opera remains the most famous type of musical in the world.
  Ⓔ The most important musicals use songs to tell stories.
  Ⓕ In the 1990s, musicals performed mainly for entertainment and even animated musicals appeared.

Wit&Wisdom iBT TOEFL Series

Beginning (40~60) · Intermediate (60~90)

The iBT TOEFL Beginner Series

★ **The iBT TOEFL Beginner**
Reading / Listening / Speaking / Writing

Perium VOCA Series

★★ **Perium VOCA for TOEFL**
Reading / Speaking / Writing

The iBT TOEFL Series

★★ **The iBT TOEFL**
Reading / Listening / Speaking / Writing

The iBT Grammar Series

★★ **The iBT Grammar**
for Beginners / for All Learners / Practice Test

Wit&Wisdom iBT TOEFL Series

Advanced (90~110)

The iBT TOEFL Solution Series

★★★
The iBT TOEFL Solution
Reading / Listening / Speaking / Writing

The iBT TOEFL Master Series

 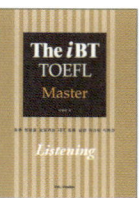  

★★★★
The iBT TOEFL Master
Reading / Listening / Speaking / Writing

The iBT TOEFL Actual Test Series

★★★
The iBT TOEFL Actual Test
Vol. 1 / Vol. 2 / Vol. 3

Winning TOEFL

Reading Step 1

Answer Keys

Answer Keys

Unit 1 | Environment

Practice 1

Target iBT TOEFL Questions
1. Ⓒ   2. Ⓐ   3. Ⓒ   4. Ⓐ

iBT TOEFL Vocabulary
1. remove   2. purpose   3. normal
4. currently   5. cause   6. disappear

Wrap Up

A
1. cause   2. purpose   3. currently
4. removed   5. normal   6. disappeared

B
removed, problems, flood, disappear

Practice 2

Target iBT TOEFL Questions
1. Ⓒ   2. Ⓑ   3. Ⓒ   4. Ⓐ   5. Ⓐ

iBT TOEFL Vocabulary
1. stretch   2. rotate   3. destroy
4. opposite   5. classify   6. strength

Wrap Up

A
1. destroyed   2. stretches   3. rotates
4. classified   5. opposite   6. strength

B
Paragraph 1- dangerous, opposite, rotate, stronger
Paragraph 2- • Speed: 100~500 km/h
• Width: 180-270 meters
• Strength: F0~F5

Test 1 Glaciers
1. Ⓐ   2. Ⓒ   3. Ⓒ   4. Ⓑ   5. Ⓐ
6. Ⓓ   7. Ⓓ

Test 2 Urban Heat Islands
1. Ⓐ   2. Ⓓ   3. Ⓒ   4. Ⓒ   5. Ⓓ

Reading Helper

A
1. It can take several months for some children to learn the process completely.
2. It will take many hours for the building to cool down after fire.
3. It took time for the group to get prepared.
4. It takes a long time for people to feel comfortable with change.

B
1. To stay healthy, we should exercise regularly.
2. More ideas are needed to solve the problems.
3. One must have passion in order to succeed.
4. Many volunteers are needed in order to make the program successful.

Unit 2 | History

Practice 1

Target iBT TOEFL Questions
1. Ⓑ   2. Ⓒ   3. Ⓑ   4. Ⓐ

iBT TOEFL Vocabulary

1. mummify 2. common 3. status
4. afterlife 5. wrap

Wrap Up

A
1. mummified   2. status
3. common   4. an afterlife
5. wrapped

B
4, 1, 3, 5, 6, 2

Practice 2

Target iBT TOEFL Questions
1. C   2. B   3. B   4. C

iBT TOEFL Vocabulary
1. protect   2. attack   3. powerful
4. rule   5. general

Wrap Up
A
1. attack   2. Powerful   3. protect
4. general   5. ruled

B
rulers, land, law, impact, woman, brother

Test 1 | The Vikings
1. C   2. A   3. B   4. D   5. C
6. A

Test 2 | Water Clocks
1. B   2. B   3. C   4. C   5. A
6. D   7. B

Reading Helper

A
1. Global warming is one of the most serious <u>problems</u> in our society.
2. Mother Teresa is one of <u>the greatest</u> leaders of the 20th century.
3. Water is one of the <u>most</u> important natural resources that people need.

B
1. Some animals leave their smell on plants so that other animals can recognize them.
2. Some animals go into a deep sleep over the winter so that they can survive the cold weather.
3. Some fish are colored so that they can hide from their enemies.

Unit 3 | Biology

Practice 1

Target iBT TOEFL Questions
1. A   2. B

iBT TOEFL Vocabulary
1. adult   2. attract   3. occur
4. turn   5. emotion   6. suddenly

Wrap Up
A
1. emotions   2. an adult   3. turn
4. occurred   5. suddenly   6. attract

B
adults, turtles, attract, season, white, molting, blanch

Answer Keys •• 3

Practice 2

Target iBT TOEFL Questions
1. Ⓑ   2. Ⓒ

iBT TOEFL Vocabulary
1. threaten   2. extinct   3. development
4. destruction   5. pollution

Wrap Up
Ⓐ
1. extinct   2. pollution
3. development   4. destruction
5. threatens
Ⓑ
climate, pollution, species, overhunting

Test 1   Feathers
1. Ⓓ   2. Ⓒ   3. Ⓓ   4. Ⓑ   5. Ⓓ
6. Ⓑ

Test 2   Hibernation
1. Ⓒ   2. Ⓐ   3. Ⓓ   4. Ⓑ   5. Ⓑ
6. Ⓑ

Unit 4 | Anthropology

Practice 1

Target iBT TOEFL Questions
1. Ⓑ   2. Ⓑ

iBT TOEFL Vocabulary
1. exist   2. develop   3. intelligent
4. calendar   5. reason

Wrap Up
Ⓐ
1. Intelligent   2. existed   3. developed
4. calendar   5. reason
Ⓑ
America, developed, stone, collapsed, upper, disease

Practice 2

Target iBT TOEFL Questions
1. Ⓒ   2. Ⓒ   3. Ⓐ

iBT TOEFL Vocabulary
1. ability   2. spirit   3. advice
4. decision   5. tradition   6. role

Wrap Up
Ⓐ
1. abilities   2. decisions   3. advice
4. traditions   5. spirits   6. role
Ⓑ
Shamans, village, decisions, dancing, eat

Test 1   Totem Poles
1. Ⓑ   2. Ⓓ   3. Ⓑ   4. Ⓓ   5. Ⓐ
6. Ⓑ

Test 2   The Inuit
1. Ⓑ   2. Ⓑ   3. Ⓓ   4. Ⓑ   5. Ⓐ

Reading Helper

A
1. Some people do not eat meat since they believe in the rights of animals.
2. Ants live in groups since ants(they) are naturally very social.
3. Since most tornadoes form suddenly,

there is little time for preparation.
4. Since deserts are dry, very few plants can grow.

B
1. Some people think that zoos are bad for animals.
2. People believe that computers have made life more stressful.
3. Some people think that they can learn better by themselves.
Others think that it is always better to have a teacher.

iBT TOEFL Vocabulary
1. method   2. profound   3. generation
4. oral   5. prove

Wrap Up

A
1. generations   2. proved
3. profound   4. oral   5. method

B
African, teach, oral, poems

C
1. B   2. D   3. A   4. C

Test 1   Detective Novels
1. C   2. C   3. D   4. C   5. C
6. A

Test 2   Gulliver's Travels
1. A   2. C   3. B   4. B   5. C
6. D   7. A

Reading Helper

A
1. The feathers are for heating as well as flight.
2. The student is witty as well as intelligent.
3. Depression can affect children as well as adults.

B
1. The house seems to be old.
2. The writer seems to know what his readers want.
3. The search engine seems to have a problem.
4. Exercising seems to be the answer to weight loss.

Unit 5 | Literature

Practice 1

Target iBT TOEFL Questions
1. C   2. A   3. A

iBT TOEFL Vocabulary
1. poet   2. private   3. situation
4. avoid   5. close   6. impress

Wrap Up

A
1. poet   2. private   3. avoid
4. impressed   5. Close   6. situation

B
1. T   2. F   3. F   4. T   5. T

Practice 2

Target iBT TOEFL Questions
1. A   2. B

Unit 6 | Astronomy

Practice 1

Target iBT TOEFL Questions
1. Ⓒ   2. Ⓖ

iBT TOEFL Vocabulary
1. explode   2. lifetime   3. unable
4. produce   5. collapse   6. rare

Wrap Up
Ⓐ
1. exploded   2. unable   3. lifetime
4. collapsed   5. rare   6. produced
Ⓑ
bright, energy, stops, size, collapses, rare, 50

Practice 2

Target iBT TOEFL Questions
1. Ⓑ   2. Ⓗ

iBT TOEFL Vocabulary
1. astronaut   2. space   3. weightless
4. adapt   5. confuse

Wrap Up
Ⓐ
1. confused   2. astronaut   3. weightless
4. adapt   5. space
Ⓑ
adapt, weightless, water, weaker, slowly, healthy

Test 1 Jupiter
1. Ⓓ   2. Ⓓ   3. Ⓒ   4. Ⓒ   5. Ⓐ
6. Ⓑ

Test 2 Black Holes
1. Ⓒ   2. Ⓓ   3. Ⓒ   4. Ⓓ   5. Ⓐ

Reading Helper

1. Technology has changed so fast that it is difficult to keep up.
2. The museum was in such a bad condition that it was necessary to build a new one.
3. The tornado passed so quickly that it was over in an hour.
4. The book was such a big success that it was translated into 10 different languages.
5. The book became so popular that it was made into a movie.

Unit 7 | Arts

Practice 1

Target iBT TOEFL Questions
Michelangelo's David: Ⓑ, Ⓒ, Ⓕ
Donatello's David: , Ⓖ

iBT TOEFL Vocabulary
1. display   2. will
3. successful   4. reveal
5. completely   6. imitate

Wrap Up
Ⓐ
1. completely   2. reveals
3. imitate   4. displayed
5. will   6. successful

B
1. Donatello, bronze, public sword, feminine
2. Michelangelo, marble, perfection, nude, strength

Practice 2

Target iBT TOEFL Questions
Fine Art Photography: Ⓑ, Ⓒ, Ⓕ
Mass Product Photography Ⓐ, Ⓖ

iBT TOEFL Vocabulary
1. advertise 2. position 3. mass
4. mainly 5. plan

Wrap Up
A
1. advertise 2. positioned
3. plan 4. mainly 5. mass

B
large, calendars, advertise, small, photographer, beauty

Test 1 Operas vs. Musicals
1. Ⓐ 2. Ⓒ 3. Ⓒ 4. Ⓑ
5. Operas: Ⓑ, Ⓓ, Ⓕ Musicals: Ⓐ, Ⓖ

Test 2 Watercolor vs. Oil Painting
1. Ⓑ 2. Ⓐ 3. Ⓓ 4. Ⓓ 5. Ⓓ
6. Watercolor Painting: Ⓐ, Ⓓ, Ⓖ
Oil Painting: Ⓑ, Ⓕ

Reading Helper

A
1. People can help the animals survive the drought.
2. The new program will help the teachers save time.
3. Taking care of a pet can help children develop social skills.
4. Good friends may help your life last longer.

B
1. It is important to find main ideas when you are reading.
2. It is difficult to learn a foreign language.
3. It is difficult to be a leader if you are inexperienced in dealing with people.
4. It is important to have specific goals in life.
5. It is very easy to join the club.

Unit 8 | Architecture

Practice 1

Target iBT TOEFL Questions
1. Ⓐ, Ⓒ, Ⓓ

iBT TOEFL Vocabulary
1. several 2. feature 3. decorate
4. shape 5. complete 6. despite

Wrap Up
A
1. feature 2. Despite 3. complete
4. shaped 5. decorated 6. several

Paris, example, Construction, 1345, 800, Catholic

Practice 2

Target iBT TOEFL Questions

1. Ⓐ, Ⓑ, Ⓓ

iBT TOEFL Vocabulary

1. prevent 2. flexible 3. handle
4. monitor 5. balance

Wrap Up

Ⓐ

1. monitored 2. prevented 3. flexible
4. balance 5. handle

Ⓑ

1. (A) 2. (E)

Test 1 North American Indian Houses

1. Ⓑ 2. Ⓐ 3. Ⓑ 4. Ⓐ, Ⓒ, Ⓕ

Test 2 Renaissance Architecture

1. Ⓐ 2. Ⓐ 3. Ⓑ 4. Ⓑ
5. Ⓑ, Ⓒ, Ⓕ

Reading Helper

A

1. The success was due to hard work.
2. The drought was due to the climate change.
3. It became easy to find resources largely due to the Internet.
4. Due to the active participation of the people, the conference ended successfully.

B

1. The drug will prevent the disease from developing.
2. The war prevented the people from returning to their home country.
3. Stretching will prevent you from hurting your body.
4. The new plan prevented the school from closing.

•• Actual Test

Passage 1 Caffeine

1. Ⓐ 2. Ⓒ 3. Ⓑ 4. Ⓑ 5. Ⓒ
6. Ⓑ 7. Ⓐ, Ⓒ, Ⓔ

Passage 2 Mad Cow Disease

1. Ⓓ 2. Ⓓ 3. Ⓑ 4. Ⓑ 5. Ⓓ
6. Ⓒ 7. Ⓓ 8. Ⓑ, Ⓒ, Ⓕ

Passage 3 The Placebo Effect

1. Ⓒ 2. Ⓑ 3. Ⓒ 4. Ⓓ 5. Ⓒ
6. Ⓐ 7. Ⓐ
8. Placebo: Ⓐ, Ⓕ, Ⓖ Nocebo: Ⓒ, Ⓓ

Passage 4 Printing Systems

1. Ⓓ 2. Ⓓ 3. Ⓑ 4. Ⓑ 5. Ⓓ
6. Ⓐ 7. Ⓒ 8. Ⓑ, Ⓔ, Ⓕ

Passage 5 Musicals

1. Ⓒ 2. Ⓐ 3. Ⓑ 4. Ⓑ 5. Ⓒ
6. Ⓓ 7. Ⓒ 8. Ⓑ, Ⓒ, Ⓕ

Winning TOEFL is a three-step series for beginning level students who are preparing for iBT TOEFL. Each step consists of four books: Listening, Reading, Speaking and Writing.

Winning TOEFL will help students be familiar with iBT TOEFL question types and provide opportunities to develop essential test skills through a step-by-step process.

Key Features of Winning TOEFL Reading
- Focused practice for each question type
- Step-by-step practice for the development of test skills
- TOEFL passages on important academic topics
- Essential TOEFL vocabulary
- Full answer keys
- MP3 files